driving myself crazy

bantam books

New York / Toronto / London / Sydney / Auckland

driving myself crazy

Misadventures of a Novice Golfer

Jessica Maxwell

Author's note: Although this is a work of nonfiction, the character
of Graham is a composite of two dear friends and golf mentors.

driving myself crazy

A Bantam Book / June 2000

Book design by Laurie Jewell.

Library of Congress Cataloging-in-Publication Data

Maxwell, Jessica.
Driving myself crazy / Jessica Maxwell.
p.   cm.
ISBN 0-553-10793-3
1. Golf—Fiction.   I. Title.
PS3563.A915 D 75 2000
813'.54—dc21   99-088843

Published simultaneously in the United States and Canada

Bantam Books are published by Bantam Books, a division of Random House,
Inc. Its trademark, consisting of the words "Bantam Books" and the portrayal
of a rooster, is Registered in U.S. Patent and Trademark Office and in other
countries. Marca Registrada. Bantam Books, 1540 Broadway, New York,
New York 10036.

PRINTED IN THE UNITED STATES OF AMERICA

BVG   10   9   8   7   6   5   4   3   2   1

in memoriam

Hazel Wolf

1898–2000

for

Jesse and Amber,

the King and Queen

of Camp Putt

acknowledgments

No one survives the roughs and hazards of book writing without a strong support team. My first round of thanks goes to Jennifer Hengen, the kind of agent every writer dreams of but rarely finds, and to editor Brian Tart for vision and faith and bequeathing me to Katie Hall, whose dazzling spirit prevailed even after taking an editorial bullet for me when I took forever to make peace with my golf swing. An artful thank-you to Jim Plumeri for designing a perfect girl golfer book cover when the chip shots were down.

My golf coaches deserve double eagles for excellence and patience—Peter Croker, Cindy Swift Jones, and Grant Rogers, golf masters all. Al Mundle wins the Golden Driver Award for commitment and results, and a big Chip, Chip Hooray! goes to Ric and Debbie Jeffries for welcoming me at their beautiful Riveridge Golf Club. I am equally indebted to the legendary Peggy Kirk Bell, Pinehurst's finest golf guide; to Elaine Scott and Lynn Mariott for invaluable HeartGolf lessons; and to the inimitable Nancy Lopez for making my golf dream come true—may the U.S. Women's Open be hers in 2000.

A bourrechie of thanks to Seonaid McAinsh and Frances

Humphries for breathing life into the history of Scottish women's golf, and to the women of the ladies golf clubs of St Andrews, Troon, Aberdeen, Carnoustie, Lundin, and Gullane for inviting me into their world with tea and sympathy . . . and great putting tips! The Red Badge of Golf Courage goes to Archie Baird for letting me play on Scottish soil with him against his better judgment.

Triple Eagle Bonus Miles go to Lou Cancelmi and Sue Warner-Bean, and Jack Evans at Alaska Airlines, Dan Russo and Sandi Lesh at Horizon Airlines, Doug Killian and Kathy Ebeling at Northwest Airlines, and Gareth Edmundson-Jones at Virgin Atlantic Airways for their high-flying support of an itinerant golfer's quixotic tee times. *Travel & Leisure Golf* editors, Jim Gaines, Kate Meyers, and Jon Rizzi, earned the longest victory walk for sending me on one international wild golf chase after another and letting me tell the tales in style.

Never would I have made it to the 18th hole without my soul sister Rande Lisle, long-haul confidant Lauri Doyle, endless literary deliriata Z Teas with Val Brooks, and spiritual latte breaks with Julie, Jim, Andy, and Gracie Whitmore. Or without the care of my true friends: Hue-Ping "Smart Apple" Lin, Pat "China Baby" Barry, Carolyn "Leopard Skin" Nilsen, Lorian "Catfish" Hemingway, Jenny "Scramble" Thompson, Ann "Network Babe" Aiken, Sharon "Bunny" Denham, June "God Speed" Jackson, and Dottie "Dottie Shot" Chase, Susan "Dog Girl" Ewing, Doug and Nancy Ingoldsby, Terry and Cheryl Moore, David Moon and Joan Kelley, Harold Peters and Juanita Doerksen, Victoria Adams and Tom Amorose, Guido and Lee Rahr, Len and Helene Dick, Ugyen and Yangzom Rinzin, soul brothers David Belasco, Chris Camuto, Rich and Clem Chapple, Gerry Ellis, Terry Hershey, Taj Mahal, Joe Matza, Chris Messina, Lory Misel, Keith Nelson, Danny O'Keefe, Eric Ottem, Tom Robbins, Bruce Stutz, Greg Tatman, Mike Treadway, and Greg Kahn, whose healing genius derailed permanent golf shoulder. A stockpot of gratitude to my pals at the Zenon Café and Marche without whom I would have starved to death, and to Full City Coffee's hands-on roastmaster Michael Phinney, who really is what everyone else says they are. A google of thanks to Ritzy "Trail Yogi" Ryciak, and Aaron "Megahurt" Glascow for getting all systems up and running, and to Cassi Clark and Jo Waldek for the best antidote to *Monday Night Football*.

Always I am grateful for my family's fairway of love, from my amazing parents, Mary and Robert Meeker, my accomplished sisters, Valerie Maxwell (whose hypnotherapy banished a serious case of Driver Phobia) and Heather Meeker (whose golf course companionship matched even her wise legal counsel), my beloved Aunts Katy and Lillie, and stellar stepmother, Zelna Maxwell.

Life would pale without my fabulous nephew Jesse (favorite golf and fishing buddy), nuclear niece Amber (favorite pedicure pal), and glamorous goddaughter, Jessica Buskirk, who can make even a sleepy Oregon town feel like Paris. As usual, overtime points go to my brothers-in-law, Scott Wilson and John Beal, and to Tillie and Chili, for familial humor that helps keep everyone out of the bunkers.

As always, the Fish and Chips Award goes to Fletch "Goo Shaw" Little. And the Final Round is reserved for Jim Dodson, my guardian golf angel who appeared out of nowhere on generous wings and made learning this devilish game an act of grace.

contents

preface

I never wanted to do this.

I never wanted to learn this stupid game. Having just spent three years mastering (sort of) an equally infuriating sport—fly fishing—the last thing I wanted to do was get hooked on golf. Whether someone was new to the game or had played for forty years, they all said the same thing: Golf is a game of anguish. One day you play well, the next day your game goes south . . . and for no good reason. That's all I needed—a game that makes you crazy because the game itself is!

Then a series of inexplicable events led me directly to the fairway. It was fate. It was destiny. There was no way around it: I was supposed to learn to play golf, and that was that. The truth is, as soon as I had my first accidental lesson and witnessed my first drive take off into the wild blue Alabama yonder—which is where I was at the time—I was hooked. Golf, played right, is a thing of beauty. But like every other neophyte golfer, I swiftly discovered that all those veteran golfers are right, because half an hour later I couldn't hit the ball to save my soul . . . or, more accurately, my mind. "It is the shithead of sports," my ersatz golf coach agreed. Then he told me to keep practicing.

While women by the thousands are taking up the game, statistics show that most of them quit soon after. Either golf is just too idiotic for them, or they're all a lot smarter than I am. Probably both. But once I launched my first drive that vanishing point of white light pulled me into golf's interior game. And trapped me there, which, I'm afraid, has as much to do with slot machine mentality as spiritual curiosity. Or, perhaps, they're one and the same. A soaring golf ball, a glimpse of the divine; here one moment, gone the next. It's impossible not to want more. And everyone k nows intermittent reward is its own punishment.

So I didn't give up. And swiftly learned that there is a very good reason the word "golf" is "flog" spelled backward. On the other hand, the word "course" carries—deep in its meandering soul—the French word *coeur*, from the Latin *cor*, both of which mean "heart." All of which means we can count on one thing: Obsessive romantic spiritual klutz that I am, if I can learn to play this crazy game, any woman can.

Jessica Maxwell
McKenzie River, Oregon
August 1999

1

. . . .

read the ball

"What on *earth* are you thinking about?"

The sexy southern underbuzz of David Taylor's voice cut slowly through Alabama's insect opera.

I was afraid to tell him.

What I was thinking about had nothing to do with the golf drill he had just set up for me. But it *was* related to the neat line of golf balls waiting patiently in the grass just north of my right foot. In a connect-the-dots sort of way, they had led my mind to a stunning discovery: The theme song of *Lawrence of Arabia* when hummed double time becomes the theme song of *Ozzie and Harriet*. In that irrefutable truth, I was now sure, lay the key to understanding Western Civilization, and the shock of this discovery had kept me hovering over golf ball number one for several minutes.

"The point is *not* to think," Taylor coached. "Just hit the ball."

I had never hit a real golf ball before, so it was hard not to be nervous. And when I'm nervous I hum. The calming notes of *Lawrence of Arabia* surfaced first. Then the golf ball started to swell like an inflating airbag coming at'cha, and extreme nervousness pushed the foreboding notes of *Lawrence of Arabia* into the peppier, safer upper atmosphere of *Ozzie and Harriet*.

Hence my discovery.

Taylor wasn't impressed.

As director of marketing for Birmingham's SunBelt Golf Corporation, he had dealt with beginners and their excuses many times. In fact, his company actually built the rookie-friendly Robert Trent Jones Trail upon which we were standing. The Trail, as it's called, is an 18-course, 324-hole, 100-mile Alabama golf mecca considered by many to be the world's finest public golf offering. A 1990 survey showed that it had become the number one tourist draw in the state. Quite an accomplishment, since a 1980s survey had revealed that the only time people used to visit Alabama was when they had to drive through it to get somewhere else.

The Trail is why we were there. Or, why Taylor was there. I was there to go bass fishing. A certain golf magazine editor had dangled it in front of me as bait to get me to cave in on the golf part of an Alabama golf-and-bass-fishing story she wanted. I knew I could do the fishing part; the editor said I could just "walk the courses with the pros" for the golf part.

So there I was, a mere twenty minutes from downtown Birmingham, standing on the driving range of the Robert Trent Jones Trail's first course, Oxmoor Valley, where Sun-Belt Golf—and David Taylor—are headquartered.

By rights, I had no right to be there at all. The only eighteen-hole golf I'd ever played was miniature golf at Camp Putt with my ten-year-old nephew, who had made s'mores out of my score despite my hole-in-one on "Beaver Dam" (the secret is to putt *between* the two chewed-up "trees").

What Taylor had in mind was real grown-up golf with full-sized golf clubs and serious distances. Surely he knew the harrowing intimidation a tiny, waiting white ball inspires in all rank beginners. It seems so *small,* so *far away.* This inaccessibility tends to hyperfocus our attention on it, and soon the Airbag Phenomenon occurs: The golf ball grows to unmanageable proportions. As we watch in terror, our gaze takes on a laserlike intensity under which the ball's pale skin begins to crumple and smoke. Eventually its molecules compact until its mass finally collapses upon itself like a miniature black hole. So, by the time a beginner actually swings, the ball has pretty much become the hole, which explains why rookie golfers invariably miss the ball on their first swing.

Would that my problem were so simple.

Taylor was right about the thinking-too-much part. I was stuck in intellectual overdrive. It was clear that I wouldn't get over the shock of the *Lawrence of Arabia/Ozzie and Harriet* revelation anytime soon. But maybe I could do some sort of mental transference that at least would make my hands actually *do* something.

"Okay," I thought. "Just pretend you're Peter O'Toole galloping by and . . . um . . . playing polo."

Britain. British actors. Polo. Polo ponies. Hitting balls with sticks. It could work.

It didn't.

I continued to stare dumbly at my equally dumb—or at least mute—golf ball.

"Okay," Taylor said finally, his southern hospitality careening dangerously near the Bronx zone. "Just read the ball."

Read the ball?

I brightened. If reading the ball was anything like reading the water while fly fishing, then Taylor was on to something. Maybe he wanted me to fully consider its position, the particular way it was perched upon a certain tuft of grass, lending it that extra bit of elevation. Or perhaps he was referring to its symbiotic geometry, its mathematical relationship to, say, that tree, this bush, my shoe. A golf-ball-as-center-of-the-universe sort of thing, which would, somehow, manifest in certain logarithmic assumptions and implied swing corrections.

"No," Taylor corrected. "I mean *read* the ball. Read the *writing* on the ball. The brand name. That name right there," he said, pointing to tiny black script scrawled across the ball's stippled surface.

"Okay, I can do that," I proclaimed with new confidence. "I like to read."

"Well, keep reading until you make contact with it."

"With the brand name?"

"With the *ball*."

My mind could almost hear his mind add: "you moron."

"Okay," I replied. "Read the ball."

To be honest, there wasn't all that much to read. Just the strange word "Titleist." It looked like a secret golf code, but I figured this was not the moment to ask David what it meant.

"Read the ball," I told myself. "Just read the ball."

Then I started doing it. Actually reading the odd little word on the ball over and over. Titleist. Titleist. Titleist. Suddenly the word took on a tempo of its own, a one-two-three waltzing gait that began dancing slowly around my mind. TIGHT-elle-list. TIGHT-elle-list. TIGHT-elle-list!

Just as suddenly, but without my instruction or permission, my hands moved! Pulling the club—a seven-iron—up behind my right shoulder, then, just as automatically, pushing it down hard, the club head aimed directly at my unsuspecting golf ball.

Then I hit it.

To my complete amazement, the ball went helicoptering into that moody springtime air with serious Michael Jordan hang time. Real time didn't slow down; it accelerated. My life didn't pass before my eyes; my future did. And David Taylor, I noted, wore a gentleman's grin that split his handsome face like an Alabama watermelon, intent on this moment of ripe perfection.

"That's golf," he declared. "Now, hit the other ones."

I couldn't, of course. That's also golf. Not even the pros can repeat their brightest moments with any regularity. But I didn't care. I had been to the mountaintop. ME! An utter nongolfer. A subduffer. A roaring rookie fully 150 points shy of being allowed into Golf Mensa. A noninitiate of such low stature that the bald fact of a pro like Taylor stooping (literally . . . he's tall) to give me a lesson was miracle enough. But to have actually *hit* the actual golf ball . . . well, it really was too much. As if to underscore that truth, a siren suddenly sounded from the direction of the clubhouse.

"Gosh, I guess it *was* a good shot," I said modestly.

"Yes it was," Taylor agreed with a courtly nod. "A seven-iron cannot be struck better. But the siren means there's lightning in the area. We need to get out of here."

Electric tongues licked the eastern sky as our golf cart rushed back to the clubhouse. The air was lavender and smelled of medicine. I breathed it in deeply and, for the moment, was healed. Healed of my paralyzing fear of the scariest game ever invented. Healed of the "You Can't" messages hard-wired into the brain of every girl born before Flo-Jo's fire-nails clawed a path to the Gold for us. And, most of all, healed of the fear that if I take up some crazy new out-of-doors game I'll never become a good fly fisherwoman.

Well, not exactly healed. Converted. The truth was that in the swinging swing of a golf club I sensed a kind of kinship with the cast of a fly rod. Something in the rhythm. The pace. Something in the Great Divide between control and release. *England swings like the pendulum do.* Or, rather, Scotland. A lift of the shoulder. A sisterly arc. Linking these two Scottish sports back to the far end of my own genetic code.

There was grace in it, too. The deeper aspect of all great timing. Dance has it. So does comedy. "Laughter is an incredibly holy expression," says Reverend Stephen Mathison-Bowie of my own dear church, which, being Presbyterian, is, in fact, part of the Church of Scotland.

Fly fishing and golf. Thy rod and thy staff.

"Well, maybe," I thought, " . . . maybe in golf, as it is in angling, the key isn't *when* you swing your club, it's the speed at which you swing it. Maybe in golf, tempo, not timing, is everything."

2

....

chop woods, carry water

Lake Eufaula stretched out behind us like a giant alligator. Up above, water moccasin clouds raised their thick black heads. Between the two stood Tom Mann, the bass master of southern Alabama.

"Ah was down here by the lake once talkin' with the trainer of the orangutan that played Clyde in that Clint Eastwood movie," Mann was saying. "An' ah noticed that Clyde was eyein' mah boat. So I said to his trainer, 'Does that monkey like to fish?' An' he says, 'Why yes, he does.' So we went fishin'. Pretty soon Clyde had a big bass on. He reeled it in just like a person, an' I held it up to show it to him, then I released it like ah always do. Well, Clyde, he threw down his fishin' pole and started runnin' around the boat poundin' his chest! 'What's-a mattah with him?' ah asked his trainer. 'Well,' his trainer said, 'that was the biggest fish he ever caught. An' *you* threw it back. He's mad.'"

It's hard to decide if Mann—lanky, tan, and 100 percent Cherokee—looks more like John Wayne or Burt Reynolds. Both, I reckoned. But Fish World, his private bass fishing roadside attraction, looks like nothing I've ever seen before.

I had stopped by because everyone I'd talked fishing with so far had told me to.

"Y'all lookin' to learn about bass fishin'? Go on down to Eufaula an' see Tom Mann. You ain't seen nothin' like his Fish World, I gua-RAN-tee it."

Fish World is a self-styled collection of rooms dedicated to the art of catching bass. I confess that, compared with the sleek elegance of steelhead and salmon, bass didn't do much for me. Privately, I thought they looked like Edward G. Robinson in a fish suit. But southern anglers are crazy about them, and, obviously, so is Tom Mann.

I was expecting at least a glass case filled with colorful bass flies, but Mann had started my Fish World tour in a room filled with worms. Colorful, gooey, see-through, plastic worms. Some were imbued with glitter. Some were green with red flame-shaped tails. Some had pouches into which you could put a chip of Alka-Seltzer for a fish-pleasing fizz (or a much-needed balm after eating a plastic worm). Some looked more like salamanders and frogs. All of them smelled like an oil refinery and every last one of them was designed by Tom Mann himself. Mann, it turned out, was—horrors!— a lure-man! However, judging by the size of the taxidermied bass decorating the walls at Fish World, we were clearly standing in the hall of the mount'em king.

A few moments later we were standing beside a 38,000-gallon aquarium filled with catfish, black crappie, bluegills, something called shellcrackers—their gills outlined in Day-Glo orange—and, of course, bass. Behind us stood Mann's impressive collection of bass tournament trophies, including one for the American Bass Fisherman World's Championship.

"So what *is* the secret to catching bass?" I asked.

"Fishin' a Little George. It's one-ah my designs. I've sold twenty million of 'em."

Next thing I knew we were fishing Little Georges in Tom's private lake behind Fish World. A wild alligator sunned itself on a miniature island. Two more eyed us spookily from the opposite shore. Being the Pooh-Bah of Bass Lures, Mann fished his Little George with a spinning reel. Being a fly fishing purist, I had politely switched to a glittery plastic worm and was trying to cast the thing with my trusty 5-weight Winston travel rod. Weird. But no more so than trying to cast a Swimming Mouse fly in Outer Mongolia, my gonzoest fishing exercise to date. (And *it* worked!)

Within seconds Mann had a bass on. I kept casting . . . but all I got was a slimy smack in the face.

"Kissed by worms," I thought miserably.

Mann got a second bass on. The alligator twitched its tail.

I cast again. My worm bounded out, then landed, oh, I'd say a good two feet in front of me.

Mann got a third bass on.

Then I remembered something. Something from the one other time I'd tried to cast a fly that felt like a Volkswagen. Curiously enough, it was also Down South. Down Souther, actually, in the Gulf of Mexico, off Galveston, Texas.

I had been standing on the casting platform of a Florida skiff locals referred to as "that nasty little blue boat." Seated at the helm behind me was Captain Chris Phillips, the Gulf's legendary tarpon fly fishing guide.

Phillips had cinched his place in the Angling Hall of Fame by catching a 160-pound tarpon on a giant garish fly he'd tied himself. While Hurricane Erica raged all around us, Phillips had coached me in the near-impossible sport he likens to "trying to shoot elephants with a BB gun." Hooking a tarpon on a fly, he added, is like fighting a runaway submarine.

I was, as usual, having trouble getting my line out far enough. My rod, a Winston 12-weight, was heavier than anything I'd tried to cast in my admittedly young angling career, and my Cockroach tarpon fly felt an awful lot like a big Tom Mann bass lure.

The problem was weight. Rather, how to handle it. Generally, flies have no weight at all, so you're actually casting the line itself by skillfully "loading" your ever-flexible fly rod with energy via a couple of false casts. But a tarpon fly is heavy. And a 12-weight rod hardly flexes at all. So fly fishing for tarpon is about 180 degrees different from normal fly fishing.

"What you want to do isn't graceful," Phillips had explained. "It's more like throwing a baseball to home plate from center field."

So, there on the muddy shore of Tom Mann's Mann-made lake, I did my best Nolan Ryan imitation. Pulling back hard, I waited until the weighty worm straightened out my casting loop, then I pitched the thing forward as hard as I could and let the rod do the rest.

The worm turned. Then sailed.

It flew so far it actually bopped the basking alligator on the nose. He opened his eyes but, fortunately, didn't attack. Or eat the worm. (Talk about your runaway submarine.)

"Theyat was good," Mann commented as he released, oh, I'd say, his seventeenth bass.

It was more than good. It was instructive. Like the Lure of the Scottish Links, Tom Mann's bass worm had found yet another crawl space between angling and golf. A heavy fly, I now understood, was like the weight of a club head. And my old stiff 12-weight fly rod, the one I had tried so hard to catch tarpon with, is like the shaft of a golf club. If I had it right, golf was a lot like big-game fly fishing.

I couldn't wait to get back to The Trail and test my theory.

"This is the lake," David Taylor said. "Out of fifty-four holes, thirty-two are on the lake. Anytime water is involved, golf gets interesting."

So far, so good for the ol' Angling-Golf Connection.

We were standing near the 15th hole on the Lake Course at Grand National, second stop on the Robert Trent Jones Trail. I would like to claim that Taylor had agreed to meet me again because of my superb promise as a junior golfer. But, actually, he just had some business to take care of there and had found a moment to fit in a quick tour.

"Grand National is built on about eighteen hundred acres," he was saying. "Six hundred of them are Lake Saughahatche, which is the city of Opelika's water supply."

Environmental alarms sounded in my mind. A golf course on a municipal water supply? Wouldn't pesticide and herbicide runoff pollute the heck out of it? Worse, wouldn't they kill the fish? Golf's potential antiecological effects were, in fact, one of my Big Questions about the game.

"Actually," Taylor informed me, "tests show that the water's a lot cleaner now than it was before we put the course in. Bobby Vaughn, who founded SunBelt Golf, is very environmentally minded. He's a wildlife fanatic. When we were clearing the Magnolia Grove course near Mobile we found some gopher tortoises. Bobby had us leave their nest alone, put up a sign, and even named 'em." He laughed. "The course plays around them."

As if to emphasize the fact, a cardinal landed in the tree beside us like a red exclamation point.

The signature holes at Grand National are the 18th, on what they call the Links Course, "and," Taylor added, "especially the Lake Course's fifteenth. You have to carry two hundred thirty-nine yards . . . all over water."

"Carry what?" I asked, truly confused.

"Water," Taylor answered.

"You have to *carry* water??"

"Yes," Taylor replied solemnly, "you do. That's what makes it so challenging."

"Boy, I guess it would," I thought. I tried to picture it. Carrying *anything*—except, maybe, lip balm—*while* swinging a golf club seemed impossibly awkward. I mean, do they have little official golf canteens you attach to your belt? Or do you have to carry water in some kind of open container? Maybe the idea is not to spill any—sort of a Zen thing. Or maybe they let you set it down while you swing.

"So, how much water do you have to carry?" I asked.

"How much water?" Taylor repeated, frowning. "It depends on the yardage."

"You have to carry *yards* of water!? How on earth do you do that?"

Taylor gave me another one of his When-did-you-say-you-were-leaving looks.

"You carry water by hitting the ball over it," he said.

"*Over* it," I repeated, nodding. "So they let you set it down."

"Set what down?"

"The water. Where do you put the water when you hit the ball?"

Taylor suddenly seemed very tired.

"Look," he said slowly. " 'Carry water' is a golf expression. It means you hit the ball all the way over a given body of water to the fairway or the green on the other side. Here," he added. "Try it."

He drew a club from the golf bag strapped to the back of our golf cart.

"This is called a two-wood. It's a fairway wood."

"Uh, I think you grabbed the wrong one," I said.

"You want a three-wood?" he asked, startled.

"Well, I don't know . . . but that one's made of metal, not wood."

There ensued a brief history of the evolution of the modern golf club; then Taylor, looking pale and drawn, set a golf ball at my feet.

"Remember," he reminded me wearily, "read the ball until you hit it."

In two years, 300,000 golf balls had been recovered in front of the Lake Course's 15th hole. Mine made it 300,001. I had dutifully read the ball until I made contact with it, but I tried to hit it like I was throwing a big tarpon fly. Apparently, my Big-Game-Fly-Fishing=Golf equation still had some bugs in it, which are what fly fishing flies are called in Alabama.

"You're chopping at it," Taylor counseled. "You need to swing the club like it's a pendulum, then follow through."

I tried to hit a second ball . . . and made quite a splash. Still, it was hard to let myself become frustrated. The Lake Course at Grand National is just too pretty. Cardinals kept threading the air. Mother ducks paddled by, followed by strings of fluff-ball ducklings. On the way to the Links Course's 18th hole we even spotted a wild female gray goose sitting on her nest in the reeds below a charming arched bridge. One thing you can say about golf courses—they've got a lot more wildlife than shopping malls do.

"Many golf magazines have rated Hole 18 on the Links Course one of the best finishing holes in the world," Taylor told me.

Of course, I heard "fishing holes."

"Then, let's fish it!" I cried.

"Fish the hole?" Taylor asked, frowning. "Well, some guys fish the lake right next to the hole. In fact, a lot of guys play for an hour here, then fish an hour, then play golf for another hour, and just keep goin' that way the whole day. Anyway," he concluded, "Hole 18 demands perfection. You cannot hit a bad shot and get away with it. That's what a great golf hole should do."

He surely didn't mean to, but Taylor's perfection mandate deeply punctured my fragile rookie's confidence. Perfection? How do you climb from the thinnest of hope to perfection? I swear, if I hadn't taken up skiing and fly fishing relatively late in life, if I hadn't already hauled myself up from the bottoms of two—*two!*—dementia-inducing learning curves, well,

I would have just given up on golf right there on that godfor-saken perfect 18th hole.

But I had.

If there was any difference between me and the high numbers of women who, according to Ladies Professional Golf Association statistics, *do* give up on the idiotic game of golf, that was it: I'd already been to battle with two tough sports and had managed (barely) to win at least respectable levels of competency in each. Guys who grew up with Little League, then progressed naturally to high school and college sports, simply cannot understand what it means for a non-jockette to master any kind of sport while in her thirties. It means the absolute difference between a brain's vestibular formation (Grand Central for primary motor coordination) being embossed with "Can" or "Can't." Years of hard work had finally inscribed "Can" on the doors of my mental Skiing and Fly Fishing Departments. Maybe perseverance would re-move the "t" from "Can't" on the Golf door. Or, should I say the "tee." It was in this can-do spirit that I headed on down to my final stop on the Robert Trent Jones Trail, Highland Oaks, in the merry, merry town of Dothan.

To get to Dothan you pass the town of Enterprise. Enter-prise should be a mecca for all new golfers, for one inspira-tional reason: In the middle of the main street of downtown Enterprise you will find the world's only memorial to a pest.

Protected from traffic by an elegant wrought-iron fleur-de-lis railing there stands a marble carving of a woman with the dignified bearing of the Statue of Liberty. In her hands, held high above her head, is a giant black metal bug. A boll weevil. This bizarre hybrid of Paris and Gary Larsen offers an invaluable lesson to rank duffers: In 1915 an invasion of Mexican boll weevils destroyed the county's cotton crop. Farmers were forced to diversify or die. They messed around with several different crops, finally settled on peanuts, and became rich beyond anyone's imagination.

And so I made a pilgrimage to the Enterprise Boll Weevil Monument, the perfect tribute, I thought, to both redneck "bug fishing" and this bothersome game of golf. With Hondas and Ford pickups zipping by at startling speeds, I stood before her . . . it . . . them. Arms held out wide, palms facing both pest and west, I chanted: "O holy roly-poly Bolly Bug! What wise words hath thou for a golf larva like me? How can we take the evil out of the weevil of the royal and ancient game? Is there a way to undo this sporting snafu? Or am I already dead in the water hazard?"

The answer came back as clear as the words on the plaque below Her Majesty the Pest Hoister: "Diversify!" Which translated into golfese means to try everything you can think of to improve your swing, no matter how strange or off-putting. Also, and most important, just because you're being pestered to death by insensitive golf roaches . . . I mean coaches— DON'T GIVE UP!

Thus, it was with doubly reinforced resolve that I strode toward the Highland Oaks clubhouse. Happily, it was as handsome and well-appointed as Oxmoor's and Grand National's had been. In fact, it was identical, which meant I knew exactly where the rest room was—handy after that long drive—and the pro shop. Within minutes I'd located Steve Harris, the resident golf pro with the hilarious (to a rookie's ears) title: Director of Golf.

The first thing I noted about Harris was that he doesn't smile. The second thing I noticed is that he drives like Parnelli Jones on No-Doz. Magnolia trees in full bloom blurred by our golf cart like scented comets. I think we passed one of Highland Oaks' famous preserved wetlands, but it could have been a swimming pool.

"*What* did you do before you became a golf pro?" I asked him as we careened wildly around yet another corner.

"I drove race cars," Harris replied, grimacing, then brought the cart to a skidding halt.

We were on the Marshwood Course, parked beside a green, truly I know not which. Harris, for some reason, wanted to see me putt. As I've said, I am in no way a natural golfer, but I do seem to have a kind of binary (on-again, off-again) luck with putting, which I can only attribute to all those rounds of early childhood miniature golf. And so it was that on that particular saunalike day my putting luck was on.

Harris set me up on the inside curve of a swooping arroyo of green, some forty feet from the hole. It was a test. It was a joke. It was absurd. And I knew it. So I just walked up to the ball, eyed the hole and swung without even trying. My ball tracked its line with mystical accuracy, following that impossible arc to the farthest point of its trajectory, then it leaned in smartly until it dropped into the hole like some kind of magic trick.

I looked at Harris.

I knew not to expect a smile, but I hoped for a little nod of approval or something. Nothing. Nothing except an odd I-thought-so look. Then we were off again, ricocheting off trees and bumping over bridges until we splatted to a stop in front of the 5th hole.

Personally, I wanted to play Marshwood's famed 6th hole, which, at 701 yards from the men's tee, is the longest hole on the entire Robert Trent Jones Trail.

"I wanted to try Hole 6," I pretty much whined.

Harris eyed me with hawklike intensity.

"How long have you been playing golf?" he demanded.

"Two days," I replied.

Stellar putting aside, there was no point in lying—I had already given myself away by pointing to someone filling a divot with sand and asking Harris if that's how sand traps began.

"Look," he said coldly. "From the purple, this is a four-hundred-fifty-six-yard drive. And you have to hit most of it over *that*." He waved a meaty hand at the gigantic lake in front of us. "So, I want you to try something," he continued.

What he wanted me to do was to hold a two-wood in my right hand, then swing it as if I were going to throw it away.

"But *don't* throw it," he added.

I tried it. Upper-body weenie that I am, I had a hard time just holding the club with one hand. But I kept trying. Pretty soon I got the swing of it. Literally. By pretending to throw it I was replicating down below the aerial swing of casting a heavy fly with a stiff rod. Inadvertently, Harris had me practicing what I had set out to try at Highland Oaks in the first place! Sure enough, the weight of the club head—like the weight of a big fly—did the pulling . . . if I stopped chopping wood and let it.

"Now," Harris commanded. "Hit the ball."

I did.

I just stepped up . . . and threw the club away. Just as with my first successful drive at Oxmoor Valley, that ball sailed, and kept sailing over that lake forever. Years passed. Epochs. Just as they had during my first successful drive with David Taylor. Nymphs left their lake-bottom rocks to flutter boll weevil–like into the overheated Alabama afternoon. Duck eggs hatched. And every bass in the place looked heavenward with stunned admiration.

After that, I had Harris drive us straight back to the clubhouse, where I bought my very first pair of golf shoes—$80 Izods, on sale, half off, symbols of my newly forged commitment to the game of golf.

When I arrived back in Oregon the next day, I drove straight to Fiddler's Green, which happens to be just a couple of miles down the highway from the airport. I tied on my new golf shoes and marched inside. Their spikes clicked on the tarmac like warnings. Each step sent shocks of raw jock power up my legs.

My first cleats!

Every guy remembers his first cleats. The hard, purposeful way their metal echoes your stride, announces your arrival. The edge of that extra half-inch in height. Woozy with travel fatigue, I heroically shouldered my rented clubs and hauled my bucket of chartreuse balls down to a vacant practice station and teed up.

Read the ball! Diversify! Throw the club away!!

But in that cool lilac afternoon light, all I did was hit one pathetic dribbler after another. Some zinged right. Others zonged left. And each time one did, so did my heart. Why couldn't I do in Oregon what I did in Alabama? I guess the golf gods don't give any points for enthusiasm. Still, I kept chopping away.

So intent was I on my new passion that I didn't notice the man in the hat until he'd been watching me, by his reckoning, for twenty minutes.

"Nice shoes," he said finally.

That's what he said: "Nice shoes." Not "You looked up." Or "You call that a golf swing?" But "Nice shoes."

He seemed nice enough himself. (He was definitely cute enough.) And he certainly didn't look like a pest. So I went ahead and blurted out my recent golf adventure, deleting the fishing monkey story and the Boll Weevil Monument, but throwing in, for some reason, the *Lawrence of Arabia/ Ozzie and Harriet* connection. The-Man-in-the-Hat listened closely, nodded often, and then, when I was finished, said:

"You know, in golf, tempo is more important than you might think. About eight years ago I was walking with Sam Snead on the Old White Course at The Greenbriar in White Sulphur Springs, West Virginia. The Greenbriar is the site of the 1997 Solheim Cup," he explained, sensing my lack of recognition, "which is essentially the women's Ryder Cup.

"Snead is one of golf's legendary players," The-Man-in-the-Hat continued. "His career began at The Greenbriar, and he had recently returned there as pro emeritus. While we were walking, Sam said there are two things in golf people never talk about. One is footwork—which is the reason why he once played the Augusta National barefoot; he said when you swing a golf club you need to feel planted and attached to the ground. The second thing is tempo. Look at Fred Couples. Or the South African player Ernie Els. They have it. Tempo was so important to Snead he told me he hummed tunes in his head when he was setting up to do a shot. I asked him what tunes, and he answered: 'The Tennessee Waltz.'"

"The Tennessee Waltz"!?

I hummed a few bars. It was awfully close to the slow, opening notes of *Lawrence of Arabia*. Spookily close to both my usual casting rhythm (ten o'clock, two o'clock, ten o'clock) and the three-count "TIGHT-elle-list" rhythm that had ended up waltzing around my head when I was reading that first golf ball for David Taylor. So Sam Snead, his holy, golfy self, used music to direct the speed of his golf swing?

"Yes," The-Man-in-the-Hat replied. "And Snead had the sweetest tempo in the history of golf."

3

....

tokatee coyote

In the Pacific Northwest we wait for spring like boll weevil pupae. All winter, the old sky quilt leaks cotton. It swaths our windows. It camisoles our views, and bundles all outside sound into a kind of external tinnitus. Even Christmas lacks crispness.

Soon we cocoon.

By February we crave star fruit, buy coconut milk, receive postcards from coworkers in Tahiti who vanished mid-week, banana peels still darkening on their desks.

The March Brown Hatch brings anglers out on the Lower McKenzie close to town. Feigning fair-weather faces, they stand under the falling-apart sky pretending to fish while secretly trying to flog spring into submission. Early McKenzie settlers built schoolhouses every three miles because children were not expected to walk any farther in this penicillin weather. I often find myself on the water during the dark side of the year, studying the river bottom for pieces of sky-blue sodium-rich rock peculiar to the McKenzie, idiotically picturing a hatch of robins fluttering out of them on hopeful wings, announcing a timely death to this gray poverty.

By April, nature has made a mockery of our prayers: The entire McKenzie Valley is flocked in pastel fluff. Yellow skirts of forsythia curtsy to the white crochet of apple blossom, the desperate pink tatting of cherry and plum. Lilac bushes wag lavender cottontails at the new chartreuse underwear of ten thousand formerly naked deciduous trees. Beneath this rococo rickrack, trout season opens quietly on the upper river.

Then the real hunger sets in, an ache for the purer parts of water. A wading angler yearns for the cool hand of the river on his hamstrings, on the small of her back. Boatmen need green slides of water beneath their feet. All recall the plaintive pull of a lone native redside trout on their lines. That's when I quit the city and away to the family homestead far up the McKenzie River Valley.

By sheer good luck I found the property for my parents when I was still in college. That was years before I knew about fly fishing, when owning land on some of the river's best steelhead-holding water didn't mean a thing. Nowadays, that happy accident splashes in my head like a riffle. Sitting at my desk, I can smell the loamy denim of wet fir needles stonewashed in mud. I can see just-hatched mayflies fluttering above the river like dryer lint. Finally, under a sky of new blue sheets, I throw my fishing gear in the truck and head east on the McKenzie Highway with the appetite of a boll weevil heading north.

Imagine my surprise this time when my trusty Isuzu Trooper missed the turnoff. Then missed our first chance to turn around. Picture my shock as we rocketed past Redside Riffle. Past Martin's Rapids! Past four boat launches and a dozen McKenzie River driftboats, each with a grimacing oarsman rowing a bloated, winter-white angler standing splay-legged in the bow like a floating Elvis. Try to feel fully my horror as my bullheaded truck made an unexpected *left*-hand turn into the entrance of—gasp!—the Tokatee Golf Club. Clearly, we were leaving my beloved springtime redsides to fin for themselves.

"Uh . . . I'd like to . . . practice hitting some balls. Or, maybe hit some practice balls?"

I had *no* idea what I was doing. I don't remember how I got to the Tokatee pro shop. I was sleepwalking. I didn't even know how to ask for what I thought I wanted, which was to rent one of those basket-things of golf balls and go hit them somewhere.

The nice man behind the counter took my cash and handed me back a nickel that looked like it had spent a few years on the bottom of John Daly's golf shoe. I zipped it into my coin purse.

"You'll need that for your golf balls," the counter guy advised.

"Why?" I asked.

"It's your token. For the ball machine." The ball *machine*? My mind filled with terrible pictures of those baseball pitching devices.

"Couldn't I just, you know, put the balls on the grass and hit them myself?"

"Sure, but you have to *get* them first," he replied. "Out *there*," he added, waving his hand in the general direction of the general outdoors. He looked awfully cheerful for having such a boring job.

It is difficult for a veteran of any sport to remember the early days of rookiedom. The utter ignorance of all protocol, etiquette, and nomenclature, not to mention fundamental mechanics. If you already know what to do, you are not plagued with possibilities and indecision. If you do not, even the simplest operation takes on NASA complexity. Just how *do* you walk uphill in ski boots? Which way *does* the reel go on the rod? And where-oh-where is that golf ball machine, anyway? I spent several minutes inspecting Coke machines and bike racks until I spotted a large, square, metal box with Easter baskets stacked beside it, the same kind the Robert Trent Jones Trail uses.

Further exploration located a slot that matched my token. I carefully placed a basket on the ground beneath what appeared to be a spout, then dropped in my crimped coin. And promptly broke the golf ball machine. From deep inside the box came a death rattle so violent I jumped back in alarm, knocking over the basket in the process. The machine immediately eviscerated itself, sending dozens of Easter egg–colored golf balls bouncing out all over the pavement. I grabbed my basket and managed to catch about four before the machine completely gave out. After an embarrassing episode of running around like Groucho Marx to collect the rest of them, I returned to the pro shop.

I felt feverish. Why hadn't I just gone fishing?

Now the guy behind the counter looked deliriously happy. I ignored him. Because I had yet another potentially humiliating problem.

"Do you have any golf clubs?" I asked.

"Several sets," he replied, grinning.

"Could you loan me some? Actually, one would do."

"Which one?" he asked. A strange little squawk escaped from his mouth.

"A metal one," I answered.

"They're *all* metal," the counter guy said. He was beginning to leak air.

"Well, then, a thinner one." All I knew was that I didn't want one of those fat-head clubs Steve Harris had made me use.

"Thinner??" He was suddenly a soprano.

"Yes," I replied, gathering strength. "Thinner and shorter."

"Maybe . . . ," the guy squeaked. "Maybe you mean a *three-iron*!? I'll get one for you."

With that he disappeared behind the counter. Just dropped straight down like a water balloon. After some rustling around and a lot more high-pitched hissing, he suddenly reappeared. Took one look at me and dropped again. Seconds later he stood up again. For a moment there I felt as though I were in a Monty Python golf movie. Then it occurred to me that the guy might have some kind of neurological problem.

"Well," he finally half-shrieked. "Maybe we have one out there."

Once again he waved his hand limply toward the great outdoors. Then he himself followed. And I followed him.

"Oh, look," he said merrily, eyeing the rack just outside the door. "Here's a whole set. Why don't you just go ahead and take it." Then he reached a quivering hand into his pocket. "Take this, too." He handed me another bent-up token. "Get yourself a few more balls."

With that he sort of ran back into the pro shop, but I could see through the glass door that his shoulders were shaking. "Poor guy," I thought. "Well, at least he's got a job."

A job with a great view, I might add. Supposedly, "Tokatee" is a Native American word meaning "beautiful place." Built on a flat piece of the valley floor, the course looks east upon Oregon's famed Three Sisters, a triumvirate of snowy knuckles that empower that particular fist of the Cascade Mountains, the range that divides the western part of the state from the eastern.

Tokatee lies far enough upriver to command an impressive cast of wildlife, too. Elk, for instance. So enamored was the local elk population of the golf course's year-round irrigated "pasture," the owners had to fence the place off. Unfortunately, they accidentally fenced the elk *in*. That first year, greens and fairways were munched within a microinch of their lives.

Still, you see the odd elk trot by even in spring. Coyotes make regular appearances from the brushy margins. And the bird life is remarkable. Redtail hawks scout adjoining meadows for mice and shrews. Great blue heron do their art deco fern stand imitations in water hazards, osprey hunt from above. The red flash of a pileated woodpecker can derail the steadiest golf swing, while the lapis loop of a Western bluebird gives hope to the most hopeless duffer. At least, that's what I was thinking as I hauled my loaner golf clubs toward the driving range a good ten car-lengths away.

And I mean "hauled." Golf clubs are *heavy*. Especially if you try to carry them like a sleeping child, which girl-rookies tend to do. I tried to carry my skis that way at first, too, and succeeded in taking out two fellow skiers when I turned to see who had just yelled: "Hey, don't carry your skis that way!" Then I flattened a ski patrol guy when I turned back because my boyfriend-at-the-time cried: "Be careful!"

Carried horizontally, golf clubs are like a stack of long, skinny Legos. They tend to shift and roll inside the bag. Pretty soon you're trying to hold on to them semivertically at an obtuse angle, which makes them thwack you in the knees with every step, making it almost impossible not to fall down. Somehow, I managed to goose-step to a spot on the far, and I hoped invisible, end of the range, and forcibly heave my clubs into the bag rack.

I was already exhausted.

I was also teeless. Tees! I'd completely forgotten about tees. Why do outdoor sports have to have *so* much equipment? I decided just to set the stupid balls on the stupid grass and practice fairway shots.

After searching my golf bag I finally found a three-iron, the only club I felt comfortable with. Drivers and fairway woods, on the other hand, reminded me of spiders. Those fat, round black widow bodies. And their shafts are so long they make the club heads seem a million miles away. Which really isn't such a bad idea, given their arachnoid ickiness.

Feeling translucently incompetent, I set a golf ball down in front of me. Then clutched the three-iron. Then stooped to move the ball a little farther away. Then regripped the club. Then moved the ball a little closer and grabbed the club again. NOTHING felt right. Without someone coaching me I couldn't even figure out this most basic of golf basics.

I rolled my eyes at myself. And on their downward arc they noticed something familiar. A certain hat. A man in a certain hat. I squinted. *The*-Man-in-the-Hat! That nice guy at Fiddler's Green. I couldn't believe it. And why was he still wearing that hat? It wasn't raining anymore, and it didn't go with the rest of his outfit, which looked like classic golf clothes—a navy-blue, collared polo shirt tucked neatly into belted khaki shorts. It wasn't the usual antisun golf hat at all, neither a baseball cap nor visor; it was . . . well, some sort of black straight-brimmed Western-looking thing. A Stetson, maybe. Or something made out of that Australian oiled duster material. It did, in fact, give him a kind of Harrison-Ford-Tees-Up look. But why was he wearing it? And what was he doing all the way up here at Tokatee, anyway?

Clearly, The-Man-in-the-Hat was there to practice his golf swing. Not that he needed any practice. Even from the other end of the bag racks I could see that his swing looked just like the perfect frozen circle on the cover photo of every golf-improvement video I'd seen in every pro shop so far. One perfect half-moon after another.

Perfect.

That terrible, terrible word. Which should, in my opinion, be banned from every rookie's vocabulary for at least the first two years of practice. Deflated, I stood and watched. As I did, two bluebirds lit on the empty bag rack next to mine and regarded me in that sweet, cockeyed way birds have. It was spring, and, surely, they were a mated pair, a cobalt-colored male and a duskier female who happened to match my new blue suede golf shoes exactly. I was charmed. When I looked up, The-Man-in-the-Hat was walking toward me.

Common courtesy bade me stare. I had already noticed him and he knew I had (he was smiling) so I couldn't really look away. It was a long walk from one end of the driving range to the other, so I had a long time to look. First I noticed his shoulders. They were squared and wide. Oh dear. I have a weakness for men's shoulders the way some men have a weakness for women's legs. Then, since he was wearing shorts, I pretty much had to notice *his* legs. He had the long, strong thighs of a soccer player or a skier, and the well-developed calves of a sprinter or a hiker. Maybe even a former linebacker. High school, not college—his face said early forties. And what a face. More precisely, what a jaw. Surely, one of God's greatest geometric accomplishments is the male mandible. The one in front of me had serious boomerang properties, lines that made a woman look, then look again. Or, as author Benjamin Huff quoted Oregon's mystical turn-of-the-century child prodigy nature writer, Opal Whiteley, in *The Singing Creek Where the Willows Grow:* "We look looks." Basically, there was no angle of repose in his whole body. The-Man-in-the-Hat was a definite piece of work.

But these are just bones. This is just form. As anyone past the age of twenty-five should have learned, terrible things can come in glorious packages. I resolved to reserve judgment . . . and hope . . . and forced my mind to focus on his hat. Why *was* he wearing that hat?

"Mornin'," he said finally. His voice had serious basso profundo properties. His smile practically threw prisms. Dennis Rodman has a great smile, I reminded myself.

"Are you bald?" I replied.

Not "Good morning" or "How nice to see you again" or even "What the heck are you doing here?" but "Are you bald?" I couldn't believe myself.

Luckily, The-Man-in-the-Hat laughed out loud.

"No," he answered. "Why? The hat?"

I nodded.

He swept the outback Stetson off his head, revealing a full head of hair cut fashionably short and spiky. He looked like a young blue jay.

"Cool," I said, then wished I hadn't. I sounded like a teenager.

"Thanks," he replied.

"So why do you wear it?" I asked in my best reporting voice.

"It helps my golf swing," he answered.

The boll weevil stirred.

"Really," I replied. "How?"

"When you swing you need to keep your head still. Everything pivots around your head. If you watch the pros on TV, their heads never move until after they've completed their swing. Then, and only then, they'll look up to see where their ball went. The hat reminds me to keep my head still."

"Kind of like reading the ball?"

"Exactly. But the hat makes you aware of your head without thinking about it. Here," he added, "try it." He gently placed his hat on my head.

I froze. It was stunning how self-conscious this ridiculous game made me, not to mention wearing a handsome stranger's article of clothing.

"Uh . . . I haven't hit a golf ball all morning," I stammered.

"Doesn't matter," he answered as he knelt down and set a golf ball on a tee he manifested like some kind of magic trick. "Just swing the club, and let the ball get in its way. Keep *your* head in the club head . . . and *my* hat on your head."

I took a big breath, stepped up, pulled the club back, then slammed it down . . . and missed the ball altogether. I wanted to cry. "You're trying too hard," The-Man-Who-Loans-Hats said. There was real kindness in his voice now. "Don't try to *hit* the ball, just let the weight of the club head swing *through* the ball. It's like a pendulum. If you let it, the club really will swing through—you'll feel it. That's why I said to keep your head in the club head. Take a couple of practice swings, then try it again."

Studies have proven that if a person's first impression of someone is that he's safe, that trust is so deeply etched into the old limbic brain it's hard to undo it later. This more than anything else, I believe, explains the amazing Teflon qualities of both Presidents Ronald Reagan and Bill Clinton (and why Ross Perot and Bob Dole make people run screaming from the room). All I know is that a sweet, *safe* strength had emanated from The-Man-in-the-Hat from the moment he'd commented on my new golf shoes. And it seemed to be getting sweeter by the minute. The emotional fallout from this fact was fortunate indeed: It made me relax. Whatever else transpired between us, this guy was good for my golf game.

Instead of taking a breath and holding it, I found myself exhaling deeply, and felt all the nervous anticipation I had arrived with dissipate into thin air. I pulled the club back a few times and let it fall into its own natural circular orbit, then I moved closer to the ball and did the same thing again.

The ball sailed.

"But I barely hit it!" I complained happily.

"That's right," The-Man-in-the-Hat agreed. "You don't need to if you let the club do the work. How would you like to go play nine holes of golf?"

"*You'd* play golf with *me*?" I asked, astonished.

"Sure," he replied.

"Well . . . ," I said, feeling suddenly giddy. "Why not!" I extended my hand. "I'm Jessica."

"Graham," The Man-in-the-Hat said back.

His handshake felt like his voice, strong but careful. There was a sexy subtext to it, too, a restrained sensuality much like David Taylor's. Men give themselves away in the most endearing fashion. "They have no idea," I thought.

Minutes later we were walking along, pulling our bags on bag carts behind us, laughing like old golf buddies. Still using only my three-iron and still wearing Graham's hat, I hit the first drive of my first official golf game like a pro . . . right into the trees. Without a word, Graham teed up a second ball for me, then said: "Trust the club."

I did. And that ball flew again, this time arrow-straight. Graham's drive went three times farther, of course, with faultless liftoff. His second hit faded left onto the green and landed inches from the hole. He was pleased.

"You're good luck," he said. "I'm putting for birdie."

"Who's Birdie?" I asked.

After we'd both "holed our balls," as Graham called successful putting, he gave me a brief introduction to the eagle/birdie/bogey terms of golf (two under par, one under, one over), breathing new life into the term "That's par for the course."

Graham's drive from the second tee was stellar. My breath caught in my throat at the very sound of it, a kind of accelerated rushing that came to a fine point in a blast reminiscent of lion's roar and Porsches. It was thrilling to stand so close to it.

The power of Graham's golf swing inspired me to try for power, too, a dangerous proposition for a rookie. Imitating his broad swing, I brought my five-iron *way* back, forgot everything I'd learned, and smacked the ball as hard as I could. It skittered out in a pathetic little grounder that went maybe twenty yards.

"I tried too hard," I announced before Graham could.

He nodded and patted my shoulder. As we walked back to the golf cart, my eye caught something moving in the bushes on the right. Coyote!

A young coyote with a glossy coat stepped into plain view. He appeared to be playing with something. His plaything held his attention so fully that he didn't seem to know we were there. Or perhaps he knew and didn't care. We stopped to watch.

The coyote's toy turned out to be a shrew. It was stunned, but alive. The coyote would catch it in his mouth, fling it high in the air, watch it fall back to the ground, pounce on it with both front paws, then repeat his brutal game—much, I am sure, to the shrew's horror.

Graham smiled, then began to move on, but I stood transfixed. That arc. That falling fall, as Opal Whiteley might have said. It was the same size and shape of a golf swing! And it had the same tempo. It was as if the coyote was tossing the shrew into the arc of a good golf swing so I could *see* it. With each throw, the shrew slowed on its ascent, hesitated at the top of its curved trajectory, then accelerated on its descent. The Great Golf Coach in the Sky had come up with a most vivid illustration of pendulous action.

"Gosh," I breathed, "golf really *is* like fly fishing."

It was Graham's turn to look startled.

"*You* fly fish??"

4

O, give me a hole where the buffalo roll!

"I hope no one can see my Tweety Bird underwear through these."

So spoke Rande Lisle as she zipped up a new pair of khaki slacks in preparation for the first golf lesson of her life.

A Seattle high school art teacher by profession (hence her creative personal effects), Rande has about as much interest in golf as Tiger Woods has in . . . well, probably Tweety Bird underwear. But being best friends, we've supported each other through more than twenty years of assorted obsessions. So, since I had taken up golf, Rande had to take up golf. Besides, it's a social game. I needed girl golf buddies the way guys need guy golf buddies. The royal and ancient game, however, seemed to push the edges of Rande's tolerance envelope.

"GOLF?!!" she hollered when I called to confess my new passion. "I thought golf was for Republicans . . . and dorks!"

So far, I agreed with the dork part. In fact, I resembled that remark. Nonetheless, I tried to convey to her the exhilaration of the game, the joy of a golf ball well struck.

"But, I'm dyslexic!" Rande wailed. "That makes me uncoordinated. I'd probably kill someone if I started hitting hard little balls all over the place. Maybe I'd kill *you*."

She sounded serious. There was, I knew, only one sure course of coercion.

"Well . . . ," I said in a voice like a greased weasel, "you know, Rande, in a couple of weeks I'm going on a golf tour of **MONTANA** . . . and I thought, you know, maybe you'd like to go with me."

I counted the beats: one, two, three . . . FIRE!

"**MONTANA!!**" Rande yelled into the phone. "You're going to MONTANA!?"

Some people love Paris. Others love Hawaii. Rande loves Montana with a passion that borders on geographic dementia. Dangling Montana in front of her was the only way I got her to go on a fly fishing adventure with me the summer before, even though she considers catch-and-release "torture-and-release." I reckon I could persuade Rande to take Limburger cheese–making lessons with me, or study the history of parasite removal, as long as it took place in Montana. To her, the whole state is infused with an energy so ecstatic that she goes into a kind of spiritual stupefaction when she's there. The problem as I saw it was going to be how to get my artiste compadre to keep her eye on the ball and *not* the Big Sky state's big sky.

"*Look* at those clouds!" Rande rhapsodized as we aimed our little sky-colored rental car in the direction of the Flathead Valley. It was almost summer, and Montana had already turned on its famous cloudworks, massive high-rise cumulus humilis coiffures that appear to have recently escaped from the court of King Louis XVI.

"They're nice," I allowed. "But clouds have nothing to do with golf."

"Well, that one looks like a golf ball," Rande countered. Then she frowned. "What does Montana have to do with golf anyway? I mean, when you think of Montana you think of mountains or horses . . . even fly fishing. But *golf*??"

"Oh, there's been great golf here for sixty years," proclaimed Mike Dowaliby, head golf pro at Whitefish Lake Golf

Club. Whitefish Lake was our first stop on the Montana golf marathon I'd put together. My plan was to hook Rande on the natural beauty of golf courses *before* we took our first lesson. From the look of it, Whitefish Lake was a great start.

"We built our first nine holes in 1936," Mike explained. "The second nine in the early sixties—that's our North Course. Our eighteen-hole South Course was built between 1980 and 1994."

It's a very pretty place, Whitefish Lake Golf Club, slugged up like it is in the far corner of the Flathead Valley in Montana's northwestern hill country.

"Is this golf course named after those lawn decorations?" Rande asked.

Mike's eyebrows went north. His eyes followed her gaze to a set of whitewashed wooden fish resting in the grass near our feet.

"Those are tee markers," he explained. "Traditionally, men use the white, ladies use the red, and your better golfers use the blue. The club is named after the lake, which is named after the town of Whitefish, which is about a mile south of here.

"There's our clubhouse," he added, waving toward a vintage varnished log building as we squished ourselves into a golf cart.

"Wow!" Rande said, her Art History Radar on red alert. "It looks like a WPA project."

"It was," Mike confirmed. "Built in 1935. It houses the Whitefish Lake Restaurant, one of the best around. Okay," he began a little farther down the cart path, "we're on the North Course now, and this is our fourth hole, our signature hole. It's a par three, a hundred ninety-four yards from the blue. The big fountain there is the most photographed feature we've got."

"Any fish in it?" I asked.

Mike looked at me coolly. "I doubt it," he said, then drove us to the South Course in silence. Soon we were among houses. Very nice houses, but some seemed awfully close to the fairway. One appeared to have been vandalized.

"Why does that one have so many broken windows?" Rande asked.

"It's on the fifth hole, a long par four, three hundred eighty-nine from the back tee. Guys try to cut over the house."

Our cart labored uphill. On the other side, the landscape opened into something out of a Sierra Club calendar. Birch trees were everywhere, their new green leaves strobing wildly in the sun, their trunks burning white lines into Montana's blue sky. To the left, ducklings followed their mothers in panicked caravans across a surprisingly long pond filled with half-submerged cattails. Wood ducks and mallards posed with great nobility beside the shorter grasses.

"Is that Whitefish Lake?" Rande asked.

"No," Mike answered ruefully. "That's a marsh that flooded and became a lake. We've had a lot of rain—a hundred one inches used to be the record; we've had a hundred forty-three already this year."

"Sounds like Seattle," Rande commiserated.

Our next stop was the 18th hole, the club's championship par 4.

"That's a big mountain!" Rande noted.

"That *is* Big Mountain," Mike replied. "Snowcapped until June. Makes a good championship hole. In April here you can downhill ski in the morning and play golf that afternoon."

"Oh good, break your leg *and* a window in the same day!" Rande replied, giggling until I elbowed her.

Wishing to make short work of the soggy end of Whitefish Lake Golf Club, and probably of our tour, Mike drove us swiftly back to the North Course, stopping at its 3rd hole to greet an elderly golfer.

"How you doin', young man?" Mike called.

"As I please," the gentleman practically spat back, then he took a mighty swing with his driver. His ball vanished. "We'll see when you get to be eighty-three if you can still do that."

"What's his name?" Rande asked Mike. The man over-heard her.

"You know, when I was a singer and comedian I went by the name of Yasihavenjokeshagkavovitch . . . but you can call me Eddie."

Our first vaudevillian golfer.

"See, Rande," I said, "all kinds of interesting people play golf."

At the 12th hole Mike stopped again. There, finally, to the right of the fairway was the real Whitefish Lake.

"Oh, it's beautiful!" Rande sang, and took a photograph.

"That's Jim Nabors's house up there on the hill," Mike said.

"Sha-zam!" Rande and I replied in unison.

"And there's our glass guy," he added, hailing a walking golfer.

"Whose window are you replacing today?" Mike asked him.

"Mountain side," the golfer answered. "You know which one."

"Yeah," Mike replied. "That's why they're moving."

Our last stop was the 10th hole, which Mike pronounced "a little dogleg."

"Is that because dogs like to lift their legs on that tree out there in the middle of the wayfarer?" Rande asked.

"*Fairway,*" I corrected.

"No, but a lot of guys would like to," Mike confessed. "You can see it's in the way. About ten years ago it was hit by light-ning and everyone said, 'Great!' . . . but it came back twofold. Grew two new trunks and now it's bushier than ever."

"I heard of that happening to a guy's hair after he was struck by lightning," Rande said solemnly. "He lost it all, first, then it grew back like Einstein's."

"Just like learning to play golf," I muttered. "You think you've mastered something, then you completely lose it and it's twice as hard to learn it again."

"I can't wait," Rande groaned.

She didn't have to wait long. We had a quick but impressive lunch at Grouse Mountain Lodge, a handsome place overlooking the South Course's 18th hole. We shared a feast of hot duck potstickers, smoked quail salad, and a sampler of grilled buffalo steak, broiled antelope, and venison in a blackberry demi-glacé.

"I feel like I just ate a Montana zoo," Rande moaned happily. "So far, golf is pretty fun."

So far, my plan was working.

Our first lesson was scheduled at Meadow Lake Resort, just northeast of Whitefish in the town of Columbia Falls. The entrance is all but invisible—we passed it three times, then learned that this is part of Meadow Lake's admirable attempt to blend into the landscape.

"The course really is carefully cut through the woods," Meadow Lake golf pro Kyle Long told us. "The owner, Peter Tracy, is very ecologically minded."

"That's just like the Robert Trent Jones Trail in Alabama," I said to Rande. "You'd be surprised how many golf courses are enlightened these days."

I felt a little like a golf brochure. Beautiful Scenery! Fun Golf Carts! Interesting People! Fabulous Food! Environmentally Friendly! PLAY GOLF!! But the truth is that it's often true.

Meadow Lake goes so far as to apply the high-minded principles of Integrated Pest Management to all of its 330 acres, keeping the use of toxic chemicals to a minimum.

"That really reduces water pollution and protects wildlife," Kyle instructed. "The water trap on the fifth hole is full of little brook trout. [I held my tongue.] We're one step away from being an Audubon-certified golf course."

Which explains why a wide selection of migratory songbirds exploded out of the bushes when I shanked the bejesus out of the first drive of our golf lesson.

"Line the club up with your target, not your body," Kyle offered.

Now that was a new one. How many golf swing concepts *are* there, anyway?

I tried it. The ball straightened out all right, but it skittered along the grass as if I were bowling. Kyle told me to keep practicing while he inspected Rande's grip. He was a fast-moving fellow, and he had an intensity about him that made you pay attention. It also made me nervous.

"The most important thing is the grip with the left hand," he told Rande. "Gals tend to do this . . ." He slid his left palm to the left. "You want your left hand all the way on top of the club."

Rande regripped her club—a three-iron, on my recommendation—then took a mighty swing. Her ball squirted a few inches up into the air.

"Ever hit a golf ball before?" Kyle asked.

Rande shook her head.

"I thought so."

"I'm dyslexic!" Rande cried in defense, as if the notion of being good at anything mechanical was impossible. Kyle didn't seem to hear her.

"My feeling is that if you can't hit the ball to there [about three feet], then you can't hit it to the green. Practice that a while . . . you get to look at the Rockies while you do."

I couldn't have paid him to be a better golf mascot. Rande was so taken by the extravagant landscape, she didn't care that her golf balls spewed forth like popping popcorn.

"Oh [zing!], the mountains are just [zong!] *beau*tiful!" she agreed. Then she spotted something at the edge of the woods.

"Look! A buffalo! Rolling on its back!"

"That's an elk," Kyle corrected. "They bed down all over the place in the spring. We also see black bear and moose, especially around Meadow Lake. The lake attracts animals.

Pretty soon there'll be baby turtles out there, too, sitting on their parents' backs. The lake also makes golf more interesting," he added. "Our eighth hole has a great peninsula green, for instance; you putt surrounded by water. And Holes 16 and 18 actually cross the lake."

"Dyslexics don't swim very well," Rande said anxiously. I reassured her that we were just hitting a few practice balls, not playing the course.

Meadow Lake, it turned out, is fed by Garnier Creek, which eventually joins Trumble Creek, a tributary of the Flathead River where Rande and I had fished the summer before. Once again, I lamented our lack of fly rods, especially given the local brook trout population, but didn't dare say anything to detract from Rande's budding interest in golf . . . or, at least, golf courses.

We spent about twenty minutes hitting golf balls. Rande continued to make a mess out of each drive, and so did I. I *tried* to read the ball. I *tried* to trust the club. I *tried* to keep my head in the club head. I *tried* to be one with the Tokatee Coyote. I *tried* to line my club up with the target (though, on the driving range, I wasn't sure what it was). And I *tried* to keep my left hand on top. But my faithful three-iron felt like a foreign object in my hands. My swing had no form at all. And every shot just zigged or zagged with heartbreaking regularity.

"I've got Golfheimer's disease!" I finally wailed to Rande. "I've forgotten everything I've learned!"

"Oh," she sang back between frighteningly erratic power-swings, "it doesn't matter." (Zing!) "Golf is a *spiritual* sport! Just look at the sky!" (Zong!) "Just look at those *trees!*" (Zap!) "Just look at that buffalo rolling around happy as a pig in mud!" (Zowie!!)

"Elk," Lyle said. "But you're right about the scenery. With the trees and the wildlife, the lakes, mountains, streams, and with the course itself cut through all this natural beauty . . .

well, to me, that makes Meadow Lake a real Montana golf course."

We left Meadow Lake in a real Montana summer storm. The northern sky looked like it had taken a beating. Monstrous cumulonimbus clouds rose above us like tarnished silver belt buckles. Soon raindrops covered the windshield with massive welts. Rande was driving.

"We're hydroplaning!" she cried. "I can't see the line between the lanes."

"That's because there isn't one," I answered.

One thing all girl golf buddies know—when the weather gets tough, the tough go shopping. So, when we spotted the "Annual Boot Sale" sign in the window of Kalispell's Western Outdoor store, we didn't even have to discuss it. Two hundred dollars later we sashayed back to the car like a couple of golfing rodeo queens. The skies, we noted, had cleared.

"Works every time," I confirmed. "Hey, maybe we should have bought a pair of those baby cowboy boots as a golf god offering."

"Aw, let's just leave 'em some Tweety Bird undies."

"Then what would *you* wear?"

"Tweety Bird undies. They were ten pair for a dollar. I've got tons of 'em."

"Well, I'm glad you told me or I would have thought you never changed your underwear."

"You *can* see them through my golf pants, can't you."

"Only when you bend over."

"Which is every time I swing."

"Well, just think about golf," I counseled. "Graham says we should keep our head in our club head, anyway."

"Your grandma played golf?" Rande asked, amazed.

"Of course not," I answered.

"Then who's 'Gram'?" Rande inquired.

"I really don't know," I replied.

"What do you mean you don't know?"

"Oh, he's just this guy who keeps showing up when I practice hitting balls back home."

"A golf stalker!" Rande breathed.

"He's not a stalker. He's . . . sweet."

"They always are," Rande cautioned. "At first."

"Well, why would he be stalking *me*?"

"Breasts."

"RANDE!"

"Well, you can see them through your golf clothes."

"He's not that kind of guy."

"Every guy is that kind of guy."

"No," I replied, "Graham is different. Maybe he likes breasts—I don't know. But he's . . . thoughtful."

"He *thinks* about breasts."

"Oh, stop it."

"Okay, so why is he stalking you?"

"He's not . . . oh, I don't know."

"Well, how many times have you 'run into' him?"

"Twice. But it was just a coincidence. There are only four golf courses to choose from back home, and one's private."

"And he just happened to be at both places at exactly the same time you were. Okay, so, where's he from? What does he do? What do he daddy do??"

"I didn't ask him."

"Well, what did you talk about?"

"Golf."

"Golf?"

"Golf."

"You only talked about golf?"

"Rande, that's what people *talk* about on golf courses. GOLF. Actually, Graham really has helped my golf swing."

She eyed me sideways. Then she dropped her Best Girl-friend Bomb.

"He's cute, isn't he."

I didn't answer.

"He's CUTE, right?"

"Okay . . . YES! He's cute! Okay?"

"How cute?"

"Very cute."

"Shoulders?"

"Yes."

"Thighs?"

"Oh yeah."

"Hands?"

"Perfect."

"Wedding ring?"

"Nope."

"Bald?"

"Blue jay."

"Blue jay?"

"He's got one of those spiky new crew cuts."

"Cool."

"I know. He even fly fishes."

"So, when are you going to see him again?"

"I don't know."

"Just whenever he shows up?"

"I guess."

"Do you think he will?"

"He has so far."

(One-Minute Unconvinced Girlfriend Silence)

"I don't know," Rande said slowly. "This game has a lot of sex in it: shafts, heads . . . holes."

She was just trying to get back at me for telling her that fly fishing was sexy because it was full of "rods, flies, and shooting line."

"I'll be careful," I promised her.

"Well," she said with a strange little flamenco hand gesture as we parked in front of the Northern Pines Golf Club, "safe golf!"

5

skylark

No one in the pro shop noticed our entrance; all eyes were on the golf tournament on the TV screen. Someone was backed up against a tree. Then, somehow his shot exploded out toward the green, landing only feet from the hole. The crowd roared. So did the pro shop guys.

"Who was it?" I asked the young man behind the counter.

"Tiger," he replied, shaking his head. Then he introduced himself as "Chad," and told us that the golf pro, Chris Newton, was waiting for us on the driving range.

"She's awesome, too," he added.

"*She?* You have a *woman* golf pro?"

We knew the golf pro's name was Chris, but had assumed a Christopher, not a Christine.

"Yeah," Chad confirmed. "She's the only woman golf pro in the whole Flathead Valley."

"What's it like to have a woman golf pro?" I asked.

"It's brutal," he replied with a sigh. "She keeps us on our toes." Northern Pines' driving range is set upon a knoll, yards above the parking lot. The afternoon still had a little post-storm bluster to it, but a piece of Montana blue awaited to the west. Chris Newton cut a dramatic figure against it, quietly hitting one glorious drive after another into that blossoming light. Tall and lean with dark cropped hair, she looked young enough to still be in college. She had a good-natured calm about her, and there was an easy grace to her carriage. Rande and I liked her immediately.

"I've been playing golf for twenty years," she told us. "Since I was ten."

She had learned the game from Mike Dowaliby at the Whitefish Lake Golf Club. "Mike's the *best*," Chris proclaimed. Like Tiger Woods, she'd grown up playing golf with her father.

"How far can you hit a golf ball?" Rande asked her.

"With this seven-iron? About a hundred forty yards . . . if I hit it solid."

We asked her to hit one for us. With neither fanfare nor resistance, Chris slid into the most relaxed golf swing I'd seen so far, and her ball took off for the hereafter. Rande and I were awestruck.

"Well, golf is all timing and rhythm," Chris explained. "You don't have to hit it hard. Or far."

She sounded like Graham.

Sensing our rookie status, she added: "Northern Pines is a good choice for you two—the number one intent of the designer, Andy North, was to create a course for every level of player. He also wanted a course that was unique for the Flathead Valley. And it is."

We were about to see why. Chris and I took off in one golf cart; Rande, to her delight, got her own. "I'd rather drive a putt-putt than putt!" she hollered at us. Soon we were ambushed by the pastoral symbols of Western farmland. Chris stopped to show them off.

"This used to be a potato farm," she confirmed. "We just moved dirt around. The views are really neat. You can see big mountains—Glacier Park and the Columbia Range. The first nine holes are a links course, the back nine goes down by the Stillwater River."

"Why do the lynx stay only on the first nine?" Rande asked.

Montana is home to the biggest population of lynx left in the lower forty-eight; phonetically, it was a fair question.

"The word is 'l-i-n-k-s,' " Chris explained with a smile. "A true links course is built on sandy land that was reclaimed from the sea. Golf began on Scottish links land. Here a links course is more natural-looking. I think our links course complements our farmland river course."

"Golf is a *Scottish* sport?" Rande asked, amazed.

"Just like fly fishing," I replied smugly. Rande was a fellow Scottish-American, and I knew she'd give golf major points for its Celtic ancestry.

Northern Pines' 16th hole is built on a wonderful oxbow in the river. It reminded me of some quiet, twisting river in the Deep South.

"Our signature hole," Chris announced, stopping at the 15th. It offered a perfect pastoral vista. Looking southwest from the tee box, we could see a whitewashed wooden fence, black-and-white cows, red barns, and chartreuse hills. From the green on the 14th hole there were wheat fields and woodlands. The air was rich with moos and grasshopper snaps.

"It's a Norman Rockwell golf course!" Rande cried.

But it was no picnic.

"Hole 14 is a par four," Chris told us as we stood by the farthest tee box. "It's four hundred four yards from here, and you have to carry almost two hundred fifty yards over water."

"How do you carry yards over water?" Rande asked.

"I'll explain later," I said.

"There's my daddy!" Chris cried merrily as a handsome, grinning, silver-haired gentleman stopped his golf cart abruptly near ours. His happy cohort rocked back and forth beside him like a crash test dummy.

"When they give my dad a golf cart they should give his passengers helmets and seat belts," Chris teased.

It was sweet to see such an easy father/daughter relationship. And to feel Mr. Newton's obvious pride in his oldest child. After all, how many male golfers could brag that their *daughter* grew up to be a golf pro? We were, I felt, witnesses to a symbolic turn in the history of American golf.

To our great good fortune, Chris offered to end our tour with a golf lesson back at the driving range. Women are the market in golf now, she told us, especially in teaching. "More women are willing to take lessons, so clinics are geared more toward women." With that, our women-only lesson commenced.

"First, you want your hands to be working together," Chris began. "And you want your grip to be as natural as possible."

"Like you're hanging on to a paintbrush?" Rande offered.

Chris smiled and nodded. "But make sure the club face is square with the target."

"That's what the guy at Meadow Lake said," I said. "But what *is* the target when you're on a driving range?"

"Whatever you're aiming at," Chris replied. "You need to aim at *some*thing. Say that hundred-fifty-yard flag out there. Aim for that. The sole of your club is on the ground, and these lines here [she pointed to the parallel grooves in the club face] are perpendicular to the target."

"'The soul of the club,'" Rande repeated. "I wonder if Eddie Harris likes golf."

"Compared to what?" I just had to ask.

"So you start with the club," Chris went on, "then you take your grip. You want to cover up your left thumb with this part of your right hand."

"Kind of like pottery," Rande noted.

"But don't squeeze too tightly. Squeeze it like the club's a tube of toothpaste—you don't want to get toothpaste all over you."

"That's *just* like pottery," Rande said, laughing.

"Now your stance. The width of your stance should equal the width of your shoulders. Your feet are parallel, your weight is toward the balls of your feet. You want some flex in your knees, which helps get the ball in the air. When you swing, your right knee goes toward your left knee. And your weight should be on the left foot when you finish a shot.

"Now, bend from the hips and swing your arms—they should hang from your shoulders naturally."

"Which muscles do we use?" Rande asked. An impressive question.

"Your big muscles—quads and shoulders."

Rande and I both flexed our knees, leaned over, and swung our arms.

"I really feel my stomach muscles," I had to confess. "Like when I learned to ski." That realization, in fact, was one of the biggest breakthroughs in my skiing career: When I felt the power in my solar plexus muscles I was able to lean forward over my skis for the first time, a terrifying event for all new skiers. Lifting from my stomach, I could finally stand up to the mountain.

"Yes!" Chris replied. "I'd never thought of it, but when I play golf after skiing season my stomach muscles are really sore. A lot of people have been told to keep their left arm straight," she continued. "So they come here with what I call 'ape arm.' What you really want to do is relax both arms and swing them like an elephant's trunk."

"Less ape, more elephant," Rande affirmed.

"Right. And you hold the club where your arms hang down naturally—not too close to your body. Swing them like an elephant's trunk—go ahead and practice. Just bend over from your hips and let your arms swing back and forth, back and forth . . . Now, take your club and let the centrifugal force guide you while you feel the weight of the club head."

"Less ape, more elephant, more coyote," I muttered to myself.

"What?" Rande asked.

"Nothing."

"Then, when you take a shot, the ball just gets in the way. You let the club head do the work."

"Have you ever given lessons to someone named Graham?" I asked.

"Graham who?" Chris asked.

"I don't know."

Rande rolled her eyes.

"Oh, you just sound like this guy back home who's . . . kind of my golf coach. He always says things like 'Let the ball get in the way of the club head.' "

"Then he knows what he's talking about," Chris said approvingly. "So, let's try it. Don't be afraid to take a real swing—women are always worried about hurting the grass." She laughed. "Just relax—the thing I work the hardest at is getting people to relax. Rande, you go ahead and go first."

Rande froze. Her eyes got the same dead-rat look she gets every time I try to teach her how to figure out the tip on a restaurant bill. Too much information was swishing around in her head. Trouper that she is, she tried to remember everything, and actually did a good job . . . though not exactly in the preferred sequence. She gripped her club, loosened her grip, put her left hand on top of her right thumb, switched, then switched them back, widened her stance, glanced at her shoulders, ignored the five-inch difference between them and the space between her feet, squared her club face with the general Great Outdoors, flexed her knees a few times, glanced at the 150-yard flag, leaned over and swung her club back and forth mumbling, "Elephant, elephant," then rose onto the balls of her feet, like a baby frog trying to stand in an overripe diaper, and slammed her three-iron into the ball. But not before her right foot mysteriously shot out sideways in what can only be called a golfer's donkey-kick. I'm only guessing here, but I think it was an intuitive move to keep herself from falling on her face.

Despite these heroic efforts, Rande's ball careened sideways in an unpleasant 90-degree angle. She tried it again. Again she anchored her swing with the odd little donkey-kick, and again her ball sliced badly. Her third drive was just as cockeyed.

"More elephant, less donkey," I suggested, trying to make her laugh. Then I saw that she was near tears. I felt terrible for her.

But not terrible enough to negate the powerful effects of Chris's peacefulness on my own golf swing. I was as relaxed with her as I was with Graham. Buoyed by this mysterious confidence, I gripped my club, addressed the ball, pulled up from my stomach muscles, swung through, and hit it a country mile. Then I did it again. And again. I wasn't even impressed because I knew I could do it before I did it. Now it was my turn to feel like a natural. Completely forgetting the horrors of my earlier practice session, I was, at that moment, so sure of myself that I secretly decided I didn't have much more to learn about this difficult game. I'd done it. I'd learned to play golf. I could hit with the best of them. It was almost boring.

"That's great," Chris confirmed.

"Well," I replied, sounding even to myself a little too much like George Costanza, "I've had a few lessons. This is Rande's first time."

"I need to visit the ladies' room," Rande said, her face flushed with frustration. We thanked Chris profusely, she wished us both well, and we scurried off to the pro shop and its adjacent rest room.

"I don't know, Jess," Rande said from behind the stall door. "I think I swing better when I don't *think*."

What a relief! I was afraid she was going to say golf just wasn't her cup of tee.

"Well," I offered, "in our next lesson let's just work on one new thing at a time."

She agreed. As we left the rest room, Rande noticed a small sign next to the door.

"Look, it's in Braille!" she said. "Why would a blind person want to play golf?"

"Probably because they don't have to see how many bad drives they hit."

"That would help," Rande agreed. "That would really help."

So would taking a day off.

We overnighted in the mountain town of Big Fork and decided to spend some time exploring. That's when we made a discovery worthy of a *New York Times* review: Nina Russell, an eighty-seven-year-old African-American jazz pianist and singer, who holds court every Sunday in the back room of a shop called Electric Avenue Books. Nina's father, it turned out, had arrived in Montana with the 25th Infantry in 1891. "He was an original Buffalo Soldier," Nina told her attentive audience. "That's why I'm in Montana now."

Fans holding lyric sheets sang along from chairs gathered around her grand piano. Old songs. Great songs. Like "Birth of the Blues" and "Let the Rest of the World Go By." When Nina asked if anyone wanted to take a solo, I pointed to Rande, who has one of the all-time great 1940s-style voices. Finally, Rande gave in. For her Big Fork debut, she selected "I Can't Give You Anything but Love." As I sat there listening to my friend's wonderful singing voice, the natural cadence of the lyrics reminded me of something. "*I* can't *give* you any*thing* but *love,* baby." I could see it! I could see a fly rod moving to the beat, each stop in the cast resting naturally on the natural emphasis of the song's tempo. Then I mentally turned the rod into a golf club. Same thing. Backswing on the "*I,*" follow-through on the "*give,*" and so on. "Holy boll weevils!" I thought.

"Rande!" I whispered loudly once she had finished and the applause had died down. "I know your golf secret! You've got to *sing* when you swing!"

On the way out of town we decided to follow the signs to somewhere called Kehoe's Agate Shop. Montana, it turns out, is world-famous for its sapphires. The most famous are Yogo sapphires from the Yogo mine in Yogo Gulch near Lewistown in central Montana. "It's the only mine in the world that

produces predominantly blue sapphires," reported James Kehoe, who, with his sister, Leslie, runs the family store with
uncommon intellect and interest.

"All Yogo sapphires are natural," James explained. "No
heat involved at all—ninety percent of the world's sapphires
are heat-treated." One can, we learn, pay between $5,000
and $6,000 per carat for a fine Montana Yogo stone.

"It makes sense that the only true blue sapphires come
from Montana," Rande cooed as we got under way again.
"Just look at that sapphire sky!"

Rande was back. And I had learned an important lesson
about women and golf. It was the same thing I'd learned
while learning to fly fish: Women do not have the mania-
cal Never-say-die-Damn-the-torpedoes-Golf-is-war! hyperfocus that men do. We are by nature multifaceted, curious
creatures whose spirits are dulled by rote repetition. We *need*
variety. We *need* novelty. We need a break! Which explains
why every All-Girl Golf Adventure must provide as much time
for shopping, cultural events, lunches, and latte stops as it
does for actual golf, or it will simply fail to hold our attention.

As a case in point, the next morning we awoke with our
spirits refreshed, more than ready for the long drive to Montana's coup de grace de golf: the new Old Works Golf Course,
built high in the mountains in the former mining town of
Anaconda, which, I had to assure Rande, was not named after its snake population.

Heading out under a still jewel-blue sky, we immediately
got lost. But the caffeine gods found us and sent us straight
to the Cappuccino Cowboy in the otherwise nowhere town of
Ronan. After fueling up with a "Montana Polar Bear" (iced
white chocolate mocha) and a superstrong "Bull Rider" latte,
we rocketed back down Highway 93.

Heading south, we stopped at the Salish-Kootenai tribes'
People's Center for its enlightening tribal museum tour, whose
audio guide uses the song of the meadowlark to signal exhibit

changes. There, we learned that the tribes had been in what we now call Montana for thirteen thousand years. And that they used to fish rivers by setting fire to beaver dams, which "attracted the fish" and is the origin of the term "Hot dam!"

Next, we stopped to watch buffalo graze at the National Bison Range in the town of Moise. Then we stopped in St. Ignatius to marvel at the floor-to-ceiling pastel murals inside the chapel of St. Ignatius Mission. Afterward, we ran for shelter—and home-baked huckleberry empanadas—at the nearby roadside Allard's Jam Factory when the heavens did an imitation of gray, poor-quality sapphires and dumped uncut hailstones on our heads. By the time we began to climb the mountains to Anaconda, the sky, once again, was Liz Taylor blue, a glamorous invitation to try to play the crazy-making game of golf.

Rande remembers Montana for its sky, I remember it for its light. Like Goethe's reason for loving Italy, the high-mountain light of Old Works Golf Course has an almost glycerin quality to it. For me, the light alone was enough to justify our eagerness to get there. This is not what you would expect from a former Super Fund site.

In that narrow mountain valley, on top of a cleaned-up formerly toxic copper smelter slag heap, halfway between Glacier National Park and Yellowstone, a truly elegant—and original—golf course has been born.

"It's the only Jack Nicklaus course in Montana, Wyoming, and Idaho," proclaimed Old Works golf pro Steve Wickliffe. "The question was, 'Can we draw enough people to make this thing work financially?' Missoula, Bozeman, and Helena are all a hundred miles away. But," he added, smiling, "since we built it, they have come."

This, despite the fact that a State of Montana Tourism Department study had showed that Butte and Anaconda experienced the fewest number of stops by people driving through en route to somewhere else . . . just like Alabama before the Robert Trent Jones Trail.

Virtually treeless, Old Works' landscape spreads out green and black before you like something designed by Dr. Seuss, not the Golden Bear. Why black? Because purified copper slag was used to fill the bunkers instead of white sand. It is sand*like,* so shiny it looks wet, and as black as finely ground obsidian.

"A good reason not to end up in the sand traps," Rande said, eyeing one with suspicion.

"Oh, it's inert," Steve assured her. "Nicklaus wanted to incorporate elements of old-time mining. Besides, slag doesn't bury the ball as handily as sand does."

Other mining features were used. Copper smelting pots the size of kettle drums decorate the first tee. Tee markers are stones painted to resemble brick, limestone, copper, gold . . . and black slag. Mammoth slag heaps rest lavalike near the 5th hole; parts of them, we noted, had a light mint-green beard.

"Oxidized copper," Steve explained.

From the Gold Tees on Hole 10 you had to play across Warm Springs Creek.

"There's a great trout hole along the fairway," Steve added.

"Oh, *really?*"

It turned out that angling is the real reason Steve took the Old Works job after a fourteen-year golf career in Palm Springs. A passionate fly fisherman, he reckoned this was the best way to fish Montana whenever he wanted. We regarded the singing creek where the fescue, oats, and Great Basin wild rye grow, Environmental Protection Agency–mandated native grasses all. The link between fly fishing and golf tightened.

"Hole 15 is called 'The Crusher,'" Steve was saying. "It's a six-hundred-forty-four-yard par five that plays into the prevailing wind. And 16 features stonework from an old silver mill. You have to be accurate off the tee; you come onto a green that's protected on the right side by water and a large bunker . . . an opportune time to go fishing."

A little zephyr sailed in off Mount Haggins from the west. Stuckey Ridge held forth heroically to the north. Bluebirds flitted in the air around their handmade boxes. A playful trout rose not ten feet from us. Standing there in the mile-high amphitheater that had so captivated Jack Nicklaus, his exotic black crystalline bunkers winking beneath a Yogo sapphire sky, you had to respect Steve Wickliffe's choice. Rande certainly did.

"Now, *this* is Montana!" she sang.

She was back in Montana-la-la Land. Good. Because we had one last golf lesson to go . . . and it started in about five minutes.

"All of my lessons are given in pictures," began our instructor, a superfit guy with the unlikely name of Jude Wehler.

Little golf cartoons danced in Rande's eyes.

"You *draw*!?" she asked him excitedly.

"No, I mean mental pictures," Jude answered. "For instance, I want you to grip your club like it's a hot dog in a bun."

Rande giggled. He was her kind of teacher.

"Now," Jude continued, "I want you to let your arms hang down naturally, then bend over until they cover your shoelaces."

"That's not a picture," I complained.

"It's visual," Rande defended. "I can *see* it."

Rande was his kind of student.

"That's the idea," he agreed. "Makes things a lot easier to remember. Now, since you're wearing cowboy boots, I want you to do the Texas Two-Step."

"Huh?" we both replied.

"Like this," Jude said, then he planted his right foot to the right and his left to the left. He was wearing shorts, so it was easy to follow his movements. It was also easy to notice that his calves were as powerful as Graham's. What is it about golf guys and great legs?

"Now," Jude went on, "I want you to stick your butt out."

"Excuse me?" I said.

"He wants us to stick our butts out," Rande repeated. She

did so in the Get-Real voice with which she has often accused me of being "neo-Victorian."

Jude appreciated her support.

"Okay, Rande," he said with a nod. "Take a shot."

Reviewing his setup routine, she grabbed the hot dog, leaned over, covered her shoelaces, did the Texas Two-Step, and stuck out her derriere, mooning Montana's blue heavens with a bunch of happy little Tweety Birds.

"Keep your elbows under your shoulders," Jude coached.

Rande complied. As she pulled her club back, she sang in her sweet clear voice: "I can't *give* you any*thing* but *love,* BABY!" Her club swung forward and she launched her golf ball halfway to Wyoming.

"That's golf," Jude pronounced with pride.

Astonishment bloomed in Rande's face. As her ball gained altitude, her lower lip dropped farther and farther from her upper. Soon she was doing quite a lovely imitation of Joe E. Brown.

But Rande's golf ball was pure Hoagy Carmichael. It flew in slow motion, the way great first drives always do, suspended in that alpine atmosphere birdlike and forever.

Whether she took to the game or not, I was so very pleased to be present at my dear friend's golf debut, to have witnessed the moment *she* knew she could do it. Mostly for her sake, of course, but also for my own. Because each time a rookie woman's drive rips through space, the path to mastery widens for the rest of us.

6

god-shaped hole

At first I thought Graham's hat was a bird.

I spotted it from the Tokatee parking lot, a small black thing bobbing in the air above the driving range some six feet off the ground. From a distance it looked like a crow attacking a golfer.

The idea made me quake. Years ago, while I was bird-watching on an island I used to call home, crows suddenly ceased being crows.

I was eating breakfast at the time. Fresh papaya and tea. I remember musing over how papaya seeds look like black salmon eggs. And how the island, that time of year, had salmon swimming all around it, gliding through the same Pacific brine that surrounds the Hawaiian island that produced the papaya, whose flesh, after all, is the same color as a salmon's.

I don't know if this kind of spooky circular thought caused the effect, but here's what happened next. I looked up and saw a crow. A crow winging across the square of sky between trees, a black bow on a gray box. Then, like a gift, it opened. Rather, the shape of the crow opened. As I watched, it col-lapsed into itself the same way my first golf ball had. Suddenly, crows were just pretending to be birds. Suddenly, they were really bird-shaped holes in the sky, purple-black tunnels leading to some kind of parallel universe just beyond the Newtonian surface of our hard-copy world. At least to a dimension different from the one we eat breakfast in. The fact that they move around made them seem like a transcendental shell game. No wonder North American tribes thought of the crow, and its *Corvidae* cousins the magpie, jay, and raven, as either tricksters or messengers.

In his ravishing ode to Cherokee country, *Another Country*, Christopher Camuto tells us that "in archaeological digs bird-men images abound—incised into gorgets, molded into water vessels, hammered into copper plaques." The "glossy blue-black sheen of raven feathers," he says, "was meant as a reward, a permanent reminder of its willingness to carry fire." Montana nature writer Susan Ewing explains that many Native American stories say crows can carry messages between this world and the world of the supernatural. "In one instance Crow even made a path from this world to the one of the dead."

Yikes. And there I was being The-Woman-Who-Mistook-a-Golf-Hat-for-a-Crow. Was this a warning? Rande's "golf stalker" comment echoing in my head, I approached Graham with extreme wariness.

But I also wanted to show off my new Big Sky golf mastery. After all, by the time we left Old Works both Rande and I were practically scratch golfers, which is an insider golf-guy joke that means you know you're good so you're relaxed enough on the golf course to stand around and scratch yourself, which Rande and I would never do, of course, but that is what it means.

"So, what did you learn in Montana?" Graham asked me without interrupting his practice drives.

"Uh-huh," I thought. "A little *too* cool."

I answered him by teeing up and taking a big confident swing. My ball hopped once, then dribbled pitifully down the driving range. I was shocked.

"Wait a minute," I wailed. "When I left Montana I was playing like a pro! Now I've got Golfheimer's again!!"

"Golfheimer's," Graham repeated with a smile. "That pretty much sums up the entire game."

Golf, he proceeded to tell me, demands moment-by-moment recollection and rejection of whatever you know about golf, so that you're "remembering and forgetting everything each time you take a swing."

"Trickster," I thought, but nodded politely.

"It's the forgetting part most people forget," Graham added. "In that way, golf really is like fly fishing."

Fly fishing, again. Well, dangerous people don't fly fish. Even the sheriff in the film *Cookie's Fortune* knew that; when the detective asks him how he "knows" their prime murder suspect didn't kill Cookie, the sheriff replies: "Because I've fished with him."

Not only that, Graham had a point. When I finally had developed a halfway decent cast I noticed that after about an hour on the water I'd go into a kind of trance. It was as if my body remembered what I had learned, while my mind vanished into a black crow hole. My casting was never better than at those times.

I took a breath.

"Okay," I said. "I'm going to pull a Tao-of-Pooh and try to fix my swing by *not* thinking about fixing my swing."

"A what?" Graham replied.

"A Tao-of-Pooh. You know, that book about Winnie the Pooh being a perfect Taoist. And how when he and Tigger and everyone were lost in a snowstorm and they kept trying to go home but only went in circles, Pooh said that since they weren't finding home when they were trying to go home, then maybe they should stop trying to go home and try *not* to go home . . . and that's how they got home."

Graham nodded. I frowned.

"Something wrong?" he asked.

"Well," I said, "if I don't think about my golf swing when I swing, then what *should* I think about?"

"The God-shaped hole," Graham suggested.

The *what?*

My ad hoc golf guru proceeded to deliver a disquieting discourse suggesting that the God-shaped hole is the inner void that drives all restlessness and feeds all addictions. It's the question that begs an answer to the old meaning-of-life question, and the answer that questions every other answer.

"It's the thing we think is missing that never is," Graham concluded. "That's what makes golf such a spiritual game."

I was dazzled. But I didn't dare show it.

"Oh, that's what Rande says it is," I said in my best Lucy-talking-to-Ricky voice. "But then she thinks *everything* in Montana is spiritual."

"Rande's right. Now hit the ball."

Startled, I did. Without thinking I just hit it. Instantly my ball was heaven-bound.

"It worked!"

"So you forgot you had Golfheimer's and remembered your solar plexus."

"How did you know?" I asked, literally blinking.

"You swung from your middle for the first time. Is that what you learned in Montana?"

This guy was spooky. Before I could register the full implications of Golfer's X-Ray Vision, Graham stunned me again: He asked me out. Sort of. He said there was a new golf course in Bend he thought I'd like.

"We can be there in a couple of hours."

"Uh . . . ," I replied. Rande would kill me . . . assuming Graham didn't kill me first.

"It's called Crosswater," he continued. "Because it crosses the Little Deschutes River numerous times."

Oh reeeeeeally.

"Could we fly fish too?"

"Do you have your gear?"

"Always," I replied smugly.

"Well then . . . yeah!"

The secret to fly fishing is that it's really a secret society. Once you're a bona fide member, differences disappear. Because the overarching passion for rod and river fuses souls faster than romance. Personally, I always reckoned fishing a river would be the best way to meet the love of your life. Trust, at that point, is a no-brainer. And that is how Graham and I came to be blasting up the McKenzie River Highway into the wild blue eastern Oregon yonder, golf balls spinning in our golf bags, flies quivering in our fly vests, both of us just thrilled to be heading out on a new fly fishing . . . er, golf adventure together.

All my memories from our Crosswater game are pink. Because the light there is pink. Venetian. Partly it was the time of day and season, the rosy inversion of an early summer afternoon. Partly it was the thin grappa of high-desert light. A lot of it was the simple mirroring power of water—there were the two rivers: the Deschutes proper and the Little Deschutes. Beyond those, Crosswater is as much wetland as land. There also is the unlikely truth that Venice, Italy, and Bend, Oregon, lie on the 45th and 44th Parallels, respectively, with less than a hundred miles of earth curvature between them. And then there is the chance that the roseate glamour thrown over that day was entirely due to the fact that I was falling in love.

My golf game, too, had risen to new heights, a stunning turn of events given that Crosswater is technically as difficult as any golf course in the world. Its USGA 150-slope rating, Graham informed me, is as tough as it gets. As if that weren't enough, Crosswater's 12th hole is the second-longest par 5 on earth: a swing-rattling 687 yards from the back tee—darn near the length of *seven* football fields—with a big blue lake running all the way up the left flank.

Was I scared? Was I shaken? Did I falter and fall? Boycott the entire event in the name of fundamental fear of failure? Nope.

My Golf Anxiety Geiger Counter didn't feel a thing. Because my heart was pumping out so much eau de Cupid juice that there just wasn't any room left for fear. If love has a direct opposite, it is fear, not hate . . . or tuna casserole. It was clear from my game that day that if there was a way to infuse golfers' hearts with love before they begin each new round, the inventor of the process would not only make many fortunes, but she would end the game of golf as we know it. Because there would be no more market for baseball bat swing gadgets, infinitely expanding Berthas, Martian metal putters, Nike Spin Control golf balls that cost more per dozen than Godiva truffles, golf books guaranteeing perfection once you understand that golf is not a game of perfection, or golf magazines promising you deadly drives if only you keep the outside of your shoulders in line with the instep of your golf shoes like LPGA accuracy ace Pearl Sinn does.

No, we'd need none of it if golfers could simply walk through some kind of Arc d'Amour right before they tee off. If they could, the GNP (Golf National Profit) would plummet and the entire industry would collapse. No one would watch golf games on TV anymore, either, because every pro would eagle every hole every time. Maybe they'd only hit holes-in-one. It would be like watching an endless NBA game with one team of Michael Jordans playing another team of Michael Jordans. Or the Masters with nothing but a dozen

Tiger Woodses. Viewers would find a Martha Stewart lint removal show more thrilling.

Suffice it to say, I, myself, played like a Tiger that day, for me anyway. I hit everything. Graham, on the other hand, played a little flat. His swing was as mighty as ever, but most of his drives drilled way right.

"The difference between baseball and golf," he grumbled, "is that you don't have to play your foul balls."

I didn't know what to say. I understood that most men play golf like they're killing snakes, but I had no idea what you were supposed to do when a golfer suffers from snakebite. And being starstruck, I wanted to help. Graham sliced again on the 6th tee—a 635-yard forced-carry par 5 deceptively called "Cupp Crossin'" (it was more like Niagara Falls Crossin'). He made a mess out of his drive off the 7th tee, too. The next four holes were all slice and dice—slice one, dice the other. Disgusted, he hailed an approaching beverage cart driver.

"Something cool," Graham practically demanded, not his usual style.

"Coke? Sprite? Bud Light?" the cart girl chirped.

"How about a Tanqueray on the rocks?"

The girl tittered.

"I can get you one from the clubhouse," she offered, grinning.

Graham looked oddly defeated.

"Naw," he said finally. "I gave it up."

He bought a Sprite.

"Is that how you know so much about addictive behavior?" I asked, once the girl and her cart departed. Rande would have been proud.

"AA," Graham replied, looking away. Then he looked right at me. "Does that bother you?"

"Does what bother me?"

"That I'm an alcoholic."

"But you don't drink, right?"

"Not anymore."

"Well, then you're not an alcoholic."

"Once an alcoholic, always an alcoholic," he insisted. "That's why we go to AA."

"Well, I wouldn't know. I've never been able to drink more than a few sips of anything. It gives me the vapors."

Graham laughed out loud, then put his arm around my shoulders. His touch made me light-headed.

"I'm *so* glad you don't drink," he said.

"Well, I don't really play golf, either."

"You've sure been hitting them today. What's your secret, Kemosabe?"

"Uhhh . . . ," I stammered. "Oh, I'm just happy . . . that we're going fishing. When *are* we going fishing, anyway?"

"Next hole. There's the river."

The 14th hole was upon us, the Deschutes slinking past its green. In that Renaissance light the river looked colubrine and svelte, keeping its own counsel yet somehow explosive. Still water always looks that way to anglers. To us it is merely a blank canvas onto which our minds continuously paint twenty-inch trout catapulting skyward in a brilliant cascade of wet fire.

In this case the tension between the surface of the river and its aquatic subtext seemed almost sexual.

Maybe it was.

But for me the thing driving it was heart, not lust. An inexplicable longing to be as close to another as possible. A dumb wish to some, unsophisticated to others. But to me, in such valentine ambience, denying closeness would be like yelling "Boundaries!" in the Tunnel of Love. When the heart's gates fly open whole walls fall. And that's really the point, isn't it?

There are no edges to my loving now, declared the ecstatic poet Rumi well over seven hundred years ago.

I've heard it said there's a window that opens
from one mind to another,
but if there is no wall, there's no need
for fitting the window, or the latch . . .
ideas, language, even the phrase each other
doesn't make any sense.

That day my heart was as open as the sky above us. I bowed
as if to pray, set my golf ball upon its tiny wooden altar, pulled
my club back like Cupid's bow, and shot a heavenly drive. Not
a very long one, mind you, but one straight and true. Graham, thank goodness, straightened up and flew right himself.

"A miracle," he muttered.

The real miracle hadn't happened yet.

When my ball finally reached the 14th green it landed
a good fifty feet from the cup. Not only that, it had perched
itself on a slope like a fly on a wall—one tap and it could roll
forever, probably into the Deschutes. Graham's ball ended up
so close to the hole he just went ahead and tapped it in. It
was good to see him pleased with his game once more.

"Poor golfers carry past mistakes with them and create
more mistakes as they go," he demurred, studiously avoiding
pride. But the implication was clear: He'd crawled out of the
Poor Golfer Ditch just in time to save his reputation. Relieved, he turned his full attention to my impending putt.

And what a putt it was.

Graham paced off the long, wide arc leading to the hole.
Then he lowered himself onto his haunches, resting his fore-
arms on his thighs. Squinting, he regarded my ball's gravity-
defying lie.

"It's a moon shot," he finally declared, shaking his head.
"One tap and it'll take off like a rocket ship. You'd better concentrate on accuracy."

I preferred to concentrate on the graceful way Graham's
brown fingers draped across his knees.

I breathed deeply of Crosswater's pinkness, then positioned myself behind my mountain goat of a golf ball. How it kept suspended at that angle I'll never know. I took a quick look at the faraway hole, stole another gaga glance at Graham, then hit the ball.

We both watched in widening amazement as my ball traced the arc leading to the cup, moving so precisely it appeared to be traveling on a subterranean track. Slowly, it rolled. And held fast its curve, flaring hard against its perfect line like Peter Pan circling Captain Hook.

Needless to say, my fifty-foot Disney putt reached Never-Never Land. The ball dropped into the 14th hole with the defining *fwump* of crocodile jaws closing expertly upon their prey. As it did a murder of crows rose from the willows along the Deschutes, licorice talismans in the ether. The applause of their caws made me feel as light as Tinker Bell. My putter glittered wandlike in my hand. I think I can say that at that moment even Graham believed in fairies.

"That was pure magic!" he declared. "Congratulations. You just found the God-shaped hole."

Yes, I thought, as had Rumi . . .

> my arrow of love
> has arrived at the target
> I am in the house of mercy
> and my heart
> is a place of prayer.

We had forgotten all about fly fishing.

7

....

the golfspel
according to peter

When I opened my door the next morning, a box of Crows was lying on my newspaper. Eight and a half ounces of black gumdrops, sealed in cellophane. Movie size. The box's strong planes of red, yellow and green made it look like a little flag from some new country.

Crowatia?

Directly beneath the box of Crows was a book titled *Golf in the Kingdom,* by Michael Murphy, cofounder of California's exuberantly experimental Esalen Institute. I had, in fact, read the book before, but on the recommendation of a fellow angler, not a golfer (that fly fishing/golf connection, again).

Between the book and my newspaper was a three-year-old issue of a magazine I don't subscribe to: *Golf Digest,* April 1995. The cover featured a muscular man in an English riding cap standing against a galaxy of stars and swinging a golf club at a waiting golf ball. He appeared to be teeing off on the moon. A long, fiery arc of afterburn flared from his club head. Beside him the cover line screamed:

"YOUR SWING OF THE FUTURE"

The story was about the revolutionary teachings of an Australian golf pro named Peter Croker, who called his program "The Path to Better Golf." Mr. Croker's headquarters was in Clearwater, Florida. Apparently, he held regular golf workshops all over the world. In this case someone had bookmarked the magazine story with a brochure for a wonderful-looking North Carolina golf resort.

A note from Graham waited in my morning E-mail:

Peter Croker will see you on Hilton Head Saturday.
Peggy Kirk Bell has invited you to Pine Needles. You
have your background reading.

> *Happy Swing Thoughts,*
> *Graham*

Dates and flight details followed. I was utterly confused. And charmed.

Rande wasn't.

"Traveling Golf Stalker!" she hollered into the phone.

"Golf Guardian Angel," I insisted.

"But why would he do all this for a stranger?"

"Why do you think? Besides, we're not strangers anymore."

"You *didn't*," she gasped.

"Of course not. But I found out a lot about him the other day."

"You found out what he *told* you," she corrected.

Rande was right. For all I knew Graham could be a pathological golf liar. According to him he: a) had been playing golf for thirty years, b) was going through a difficult divorce, and c) played golf constantly these days to help him deal with the resulting stress. Which explained why he seemed to be the ubiquitous golfer.

"That's fine," Rande said. "But it doesn't explain why he hasn't asked you out in public yet. Showing up accidentally at golf courses, E-mail, leaving stuff on your doorstep, and now he's sending you to some weird out-of-state golf town. It's just too . . . secretive. It could be a trick. I don't like it."

"Well, I think it's romantic." I pouted.

"You think everything's romantic. You probably think *golf's* romantic!"

Uh-oh. I hadn't even shared my Crosswater experience with her.

"And he's *still* a stranger," Rande went on.

"Glen was a stranger when you let him fly up to meet you," I countered.

"But he was *your friend*."

That was true. I had known Glen for years before I introduced them. In fact, I didn't just "introduce" them. I had been inspired to bring them together like lightning striking from within. A voice might as well have said: "As Part of Your Karmic Duty This Lifetime You Will Introduce Glen to Rande."

Glen and I were residents of Santa Barbara, California, at the time. Rande lived in Portland, Oregon. After I described Rande to Glen he had three dreams in a row about a woman with curly blond hair. When I showed him Rande's photograph he said simply, "That's her." He was on a plane to Portland the following weekend. That was in 1984; they've been together ever since.

"Okay, then go," Rande said finally. "I don't want you to blow your chance at finding the love of your life, but I still don't understand why he's sending you on this wild-goose golf chase. What if he shows up at the airport . . . and attacks you with a golf club!"

"*Rande!!*"

"And who is Peter Croker, anyway? Sounds like a frog."

If you want men to talk to you when you're traveling—and talk to you and talk to you—just pull out a book with the word "golf" in its title. If I hadn't already read three-quarters of *Golf in the Kingdom* before I started my trip, I never would have finished it in time for my lesson with Peter Croker.

On my Alaska Airlines flight to Portland I was seated beside Tim Arky, a lively young man from Flagstaff, Arizona. First he told me about Alaska Airlines' great Arizona golf packages. Then he said he'd been playing golf for eight years. On his very first round he shot a 90. (A 90!!) He then proceeded to illustrate the purpose of the male Y chromosome, whose existence explains Y all guys can remember any sports game they ever watched or participated in, play by play, regardless of how many years have passed.

"I had just been accepted to college," he recalled. "Went to a golf course with a buddy who told me, 'Hit that three-wood off the carpet.' I didn't use a tee . . . and I swept it. Boom. Drove it two hundred twenty-five yards. It was a par four, three hundred fifty-four yards. I had sixty to eighty yards to the pin. I birdied my first hole ever, ever, ever."

Tim hit that three-wood all day. He was a natural. His first golf year was great.

"But the next four years were difficult. We were playing thirty, thirty-five rounds every year. In college we played thirty-six, fifty-five, seventy-two holes a day."

(The Y chromosome is also Y guys can remember the actual *numbers* of a game years after it was played, an ability women find bizarre.)

"So," I asked, "why didn't you play as well as you did your first year?"

"The left side of my brain took over," said Tim. "Here's how I figured out my game: I worked at a golf course—Eldon Hills in Flagstaff. Drove that little cart around picking up golf balls. I *lived* golf. Then I met a gentleman who told me to put a tee twelve inches behind the real tee in a perfectly straight line, and another tee a foot in front. 'Memorize those two feet,' he told me. 'Don't think about anything else.' The other thing he said was to always pretend you're on the course when you're at the driving range. Make up a game in your head. Visualize it while you're practicing."

"Shivas Irons is always saying that!" I half-yelled, meaning the mystical golf coach in *Golf in the Kingdom:* "The most basic kind of meditation during a round of golf is the visualization of our shot as we stand up to the ball. An image in our mind can become an irresistible path."

Tim grinned and nodded. "He's right," he said. Then he asked me why I was flying all the way from Oregon to the Carolinas just to take a golf lesson. I uhhhed and ummmed for a few moments, then just blurted out the story of meeting Graham on a golf course back home.

Tim laughed.

"Be careful," he advised. "I have an ex-girlfriend, Laurie, who went with my folks to the Phoenix Open in 1994. They were standing on the fairway. Tom Purtzer was playing; he hit it into the fringe. He walked over, they made eye contact, he slid her his phone number . . . it was love at first sight. They're on their second baby now."

On my flight from Portland to Chicago I had the whole row to myself and was able to read the last chapter of *Golf in the Kingdom.* So profound was its message that I wandered through Chicago's O'Hare Airport toward my final flight like a recently bonked cartoon character with stars circling her head.

At the book's heart is the brilliant Scottish golf guru Shivas Irons, whose name sounded to me like a nom de plume for a whiskey-besotted golf writer. Murphy insists Shivas Irons is the man's honest-to-God given name. As most golf readers know by now, in a single one-night-golf-stand (they played golf somewhere in Scotland and talked all night in June of 1956), Irons imparts to Murphy the Secrets of the Game, notably something called "True Gravity." True Gravity was supposed to be a term for "the deeper lines of force, the deeper structure of the universe." "But," Irons told Murphy, shaking a finger at him, "ye can only know wha' it is by livin' into it yersel'—ye must go into the heart o' it, *right to the heart o' it.*"

I had no idea what he meant. It sounded like some kind of golf feng shui that was even weirder than the inherent weirdness of golf. Did it mean some kind of heightened awareness of golf swing physics? Could it be referring to something like Einstein's ill-fated Unified Field Theory . . . as applied to an out-there connection between the hole and the tee? Or was it simply about being well anchored in one's golf stance by the sheer weight of personal confidence? Whatever it was, it's a miracle that I managed to find my flight to Savannah at all. Naturally, when I did, I was seated beside yet another Serious Golfer.

C. E. Schauman of Rochester, New York. Age eighty-six. Reached the quarterfinals of New York State's Junior Tournament in 1929. Won the Brook-Lea Country Club Father and Sons Tournament with his dad in 1930. Led the Western New York Open ("For the first nine holes I was one under par") and the long-driving contest at the Oak Hill Country Club in 1933. Shot his age five years ago in Sun City, Arizona, and had recently shot the lowest score there while playing with his children and their spouses.

"They can hit the ball three hundred yards . . . but they're wild. I don't hit it like I used to, but I hit it straight. And don't forget I was eighty-five at the time."

He'd only taken one half-hour lesson in his life.

"I studied golf on my own," he told me as our jet bucked its way through tornado weather. "When I was off my game the pro at Oak Hill there wanted to change everything. I said, 'To hell with that.' I never practiced, either. I just wanted to go out and play."

Mr. Schauman's words of wisdom to a golf rookie? Watch golf on TV.

"Watch their form—you know, their rhythm. Try to swing the same way every time. Keep your eye on the *back* of the ball. And most of all," he concluded, shaking a Shivas Irons finger at me, "*don't* force it."

A dark funnel of golf advice began twisting in my head. Read the ball. Keep your eye on the back of the ball. Keep your head still. Keep your head in the club head. Let the club do the work. Throw the club away. The club is a tube of tooth-paste. The club is a hot dog in a bun. Let your hands work together. Use your big muscles. Less ape, more elephant, and God forbid, no donkey! Memorize the two feet in front of you, visualize your golf shot, and somehow find True Gravity's invisible lines of force . . . *but don't force it!*

Holy moley.

Outside my hotel room on Hilton Head that night, the At-lantic attacked the coast of South Carolina with vicious white fangs. A few dozen miles away tornadoes cut a new highway across Georgia. Things that had recently been se-cured flapped wildly in the wind, and trees moaned in all di-rections. I knew how they felt.

Peter Croker didn't smile when we met. He didn't look at me either. He looked *into* me. I suspected he at least could read secret golf paranoias, if not auras. Nonetheless, his words seemed normal enough. In fact, he sounded like he was on TV.

"Here we are at Belfair," he sort of announced, "on a beautiful golf course next to Hilton Head Island. This is go-ing to be a first lesson in our program, the Path to Better Golf."

He also sounded exactly like my fly fishing coach, Guido Rahr, the first time I heard him speak. And he *was* on TV. (We were salmon fishing in Outer Mongolia and Guido was making a scouting video for *National Geographic*.)

"We always videotape our lessons," said Peter Croker, apropos of nothing.

So he *could* read minds. I was charmed. His classroom was equally charming. It was a hangar, really, a metal outbuilding attached to a set of elegant front offices run by Peter's brilliantly energetic business and teaching partner, Cindy Swift Jones. All of it was set upon the grand, green grounds of Belfair Golf Course, onto which the wide hangar door opened. So, you stood inside, protected from tornadoes and other climatic nuisances, yet energized by the rich, sulking air, and you hit golf balls out into the natural beauty of the coastal Southeast picketed by egret flybys and dragonfly buzzes. Meanwhile, a luna moth the size of a small bird flapped endlessly against the small window far above your head. I loved it. Peter's calm voice soon drew me into more purposeful work.

"All right," Peter began, his Australian accent turning "all" into "aow." "You've played on the driving range, you've seen a golf ball launched into the stratosphere, you've had a bit of a shot, but nothing serious yet."

"Nothing," I agreed.

"So essentially you're brand new."

"To any formal training, I am."

"Good," Peter concluded, "because what we want to do is build your golf swing from the ground up."

But first, he built something for which I will remain indebted to him forever: Peter Croker gave me a beautifully comprehensive, mercifully demystifying treatise on the game of golf, delivered with the kind of patient detail few rookies ever receive in one fell . . . swing.

"Normally a game of golf consists of eighteen different-length holes," he began. "Each hole has a teeing area where you hit down a fairway. A fairway has hazards, like fairway bunkers—sand bunkers—water hazards, and roughs. They put all these things out there to make golf more interesting. But you *can* control the ball from the teeing ground, all the way down the fairway, knock it onto the green and then roll the ball in the hole with the putter. That is the goal in golf."

Peter then explained that on a par 3 you are expected to get on the green in one shot. I didn't know that. Then he said that the game of golf allows you two putts per hole. I didn't know that, either. A par 4, he said, allots you two shots to get on the green, and two putts. And a par 5 gives you three shots to the green and two putts. I didn't know any of this.

"The basic idea," Peter continued, "is that when you get to the green you can really lower your score if you can make the hole in one shot. A sound short game can conceivably take eighteen shots off your score straightaway. Of course, if you turn two putts into three you can *add* eighteen points to your score. So it's a very important part of the game."

Next Peter gave me an equally basic and appreciated lesson in golf club design.

"Let's look in that golf bag there," he said. "Aow right, the first thing to know is that the higher the number of the club, the more the loft—that's the angle on the face. With more loft the club hits the ball higher and is good for hitting off the fairway grass when you want to hit the ball a long distance. [He pulled out an iron.] Now, this is a three-iron. The loft on a three-iron is normally roundabout twenty-three degrees. Two-iron's normally about twenty degrees, four-iron's about twenty-six. That's the angle that faces to the vertical line."

For one dizzying minute I felt as though I were trying to learn chess again, a game whose mechanics never failed to flummox me.

"So," Peter continued, "as you get down to the wedges, you can see the sharper angle—the ball's going to go up higher. More lofted clubs are also shorter," he added, "and each club is designed to hit the ball at approximately an eight- to ten-yard variance from the next club."

I had no idea. Peter also told me that in the beginning it's much easier to learn with an iron than a wood.

"The longer the club, the more leverage, the more power," he told me, "but it's also farther away from you, so more skill is needed."

Happily, on Peter Croker's Path to Better Golf, a golfer uses the same swing at all times—even the putting technique is the same as full-swing technique, Peter informed me, "just in miniature. Actually," he added, glancing at me sidelong, "while practicing putting you'll be improving your driving. So you don't have to learn different swings for different clubs."

What a relief.

"Now," he continued, "the impact area is key in golf. The moment of contact with the ball. Before you hit a golf shot . . ." Peter paused and regarded me for a second. "What made you want to play golf?" he asked.

"Destiny," I sighed. I explained the sequence of events, then surprised myself by adding: "I really want to be good at this game."

"That's the only way to attack it," Peter said with an approving nod. And with that, my official golf intensive began. First Peter wanted to see my grip and my golf swing. He asked me to hit a ball and handed me a pitching wedge. I stepped onto the AstroTurf. Would I *ever* feel unselfconscious standing in front of a golf ball?

"With a pitching wedge you don't do a full swing, right?" I asked.

"Just do whatever you feel comfortable with—just a small shot."

Comfortable? That would have been getting off of that AstroTurf and going to a bookstore. Time crawled by. I hovered.

"It still all feels so uncomfortable," I confessed.

Peter said nothing.

"Just a little shot, right?" I asked. It sounded more like pleading.

"Yeah."

"Okay," I said . . . and completely froze. Peter knew it instantly.

"Tell you what," he said, "just have a practice swing. Just try to hit that tee."

I took a breath, then took a halfhearted, lame swat . . . and missed the tee entirely.

"That's close," Peter said.

I swung again and this time hit it, thank God.

"Good. Do it one more time. You hit it three times in a row, you get a golf ball."

I did. Peter placed a golf ball on the tee.

"Now you're just going to do the same thing. Same as before."

Encouraged, I took a slightly more aggressive shot . . . and hit the ball.

"Hey," Peter said. "Up in the air. Okay. Now the ball went up in the air, a little bit to the right. So what would be the reason the ball would go to the right?"

"The club face was pointing that way?"

"Yeah. So just take your grip. [Peter knelt down on one knee and grasped the shaft of my club.] In golf we want the wrist to be on top. [He moved my wrist over until it rested on top of the club.] So now it's like a hammer—you're going to hammer *down*. That's how you hit an iron. And try to put your mind in the club head."

He sounded just like Graham.

Peter took my hands and pulled the club through, smacking the ball perfectly straight.

"If you put your mind in the club head, everything else will fall into place. Now you do it."

Peter placed the ball on the tee and I smacked it all by myself, straight and true.

"Where'd the ball go?"

"Straight forward."

"How about that."

"I think the grip really helps."

"Yep, the grip's key. There are a few basic fundamentals you need to have. One is grip, another one is the stance. And once you've got that, then you basically just hit the ball. Hold your hand out, please."

To my surprise, Peter took a blue marker to my open palm and proceeded to mark it up with mysterious lines and dots designed to remind me which parts go where in a proper Peter Croker Golf Grip.

"This'll come off in two or three years," he said. "And there's your life line," he added as an afterthought. "Good and long."

"Until here," I said, pointing to a snake-tongue fork near my wrist, "which is when I took up golf."

"Goes on forever," Peter countered. He was, I noted, quite serious.

"Okay, so now we're going to connect those with dots. That's why hands are made this way."

"For golf?"

"Yeah, God's a golfer. She's pretty good, too. If we educate our hands," he added, "we don't have to worry about much else."

Next he "adjusted" my stance. He had me splay my feet a little because it "makes it easier to turn" (it did). He had me bend over from the hips a little and unlock my knees some, then he told me to stand farther back from the ball until I felt as though I could barely reach it.

"Really?"

"Yeah. You don't want to get cramped, you want to feel like you're stretched. The idea is that *you* stay up and the club head goes down."

I followed his instructions.

"That's it," Peter declared. "That's called a golf stance. You should feel quite balanced on your feet, springy in your legs, and very relaxed from the waist up. Is that how it feels?"

"Well," I replied, "it feels . . . new."

How I longed for the day when it didn't. When a golf club felt as natural in my hands as a fly rod. Or a telephone. Or a dance partner. Of course, there's just no way to get through the awkward stage of learning something new other than to just get through it. And as anyone who's tried to master anything knows, once you've got the fundamentals down, there lies before you, flat and uneventful as yesterday's bath towel, the Great Plateau, that forever plain of ponderous practice.

With my golf master at my side, I tried *very* hard to love the New Golfer's Plateau. I worked at "putting my head in the club head" and swinging my three-iron "like a hammer." When I managed to hit the rubber tee, I tried to relish the satisfying pop it made instead of wondering when I'd hear it again. Eventually, something occurred to me, perhaps one of the growth spurts author George Leonard often mentions in his wonderful book called *Mastery*: I'd made a certain mental connection with this hammering-down business.

"It's like a pinch, almost, isn't it?" I asked.

"Yeah, that's it," Peter replied.

I pulled my club back and slammed it straight down, seriously pinching the waiting golf ball . . . and it shot out of the hangar door.

Peter nodded. "Where'd the ball go?"

"Straight out there!" I sang out with genuine confidence.

"Straight," Peter repeated. "That's pretty interesting. It went straight. Did you try to hit it straight, or did you just try to hit it?"

"I didn't try to do *anything* but hit it."

"Let's have a look at this on the replay," he said, and we walked over to the television monitor.

Oh, ugh. Now I had to see myself on TV.

"That's you," Peter said, nodding at my image taking a golf swing in perfect slow motion. He clicked something and I suddenly had a circle around my head.

"See, you didn't try to keep your head down. It just stayed at the same level.[My head didn't move out of the circle.] You just watched the ball. Just like any other sport—keep your eye on the ball. When that man said to you, 'Read the ball,' what he was really saying was 'Keep your eye on the ball.' The head is not important. If you throw that club head at the ball, your head will stay where it's supposed to. So you don't have to think about your head."

"Kind of like Graham's hat," I mused.

"What?" Peter asked.

"Oh, well . . . my, um, golf coach back home—the one who sent me here—well, he wears a hat to remember to keep his head still without having to think about it."

"That's good," Peter replied. "The hat unconsciously reminds his brain that he doesn't have to think about his head."

I frowned. Peter was beginning to sound like Shivas Irons. Were *all* golf teachers this obtuse? Did logic *always* eventually disappear into some crow-hole in their minds?

Before I could ask, Peter hit a button and I disappeared from the video screen! Only the white circle hung in the air where my head had been, a perfect halo encircling nothing.

I called Rande from my hotel room that night, just to check in.

"So, did he show up?" she asked right away.

"Did who show up?"

"The Golf Stalker."

"Of course not," I answered, but my psychic friend caught the thinnest undercurrent of disappointment.

"And you were hoping he would, right?"

"Well . . . ," I stalled, knowing it would do no good. "It's kind of lonely out here."

"Perfect scene for a crime," Rande offered.

"Oh, would you just *stop* it?"

As always, she had me laughing. If you can't travel with your best friend, then the next best thing is hearing her voice on the phone when you're stuck by yourself in some godforsaken hotel room. Suddenly, your life comes back into focus and you're only away from home on a long leash, not floating dangerously on the edge of some unknown universe.

I threw open my patio doors to the dark, holy night and let the drum solo of the angry Atlantic crash through my room. Thanks to Rande it now sounded like cartoon music. Then I replayed the video on my TV. When I got to the empty, floating halo at the end, I accidentally hit the wrong button rather than "rewind" and suddenly Dave Letterman was on the screen saying: ". . . and today is the one hundred fifty-sixth birthday of the donut." A big salute to nothing? A circle around a circle of air? Were the golf gods playing a little joke on me?

Or could it mean that I was destined, someday, to hit a hole-in-one?

8

....

pushing iron

On the Atlantic Coast, dawn doesn't break, it breaks in, a mobster in a yellow suit shooting its way into the bedroom, harsh, in-your-face, and demanding action . . . now! Back home in western Oregon, sunny days don't pack that kind of heat until late afternoon, when you're about ready to abandon your desk for the river or the golf course anyway. But on Hilton Head, people were jogging on the beach at 6 A.M., laminated in sunscreen against the brutal late spring light.

Needless to say, I was early for my golf lesson.

Apparently, the storm had self-destructed sometime during the night, taking with it a few prisoners. Patio furniture was rearranged on lawns in most un-vacation-like configurations (I spotted one chaise longue affixed to the trunk of a loblolly pine like a Locust from Another Planet). Much of what had, until recently, been up in the air was now on the ground—I dodged oak branches and palm fronds during the entire twenty-minute drive off the island and back to Belfair.

Peter was in great spirits. He greeted me with his usual nerve-wracking unsmiling intensity, looking quite dashing in his white riding cap and classic golf togs. He ushered me into the golf hangar and dove into the business at hand: my budding golf swing.

"Before you start your putting instruction with Cindy, we're going to review what we learned yesterday, and we're going to give you just a little bit of the basic motion of golf."

He didn't say the "action" or "form" or "business" of golf; he said "motion." The dominant dance-loving side of my brain answered "amen." But I was allowed only several nanoseconds of comfort, because Peter immediately stepped onto the practice turf and did a startling thing. Taking a pitching wedge in a firm golf grip, he held it aloft directly in front of him and stared at its far end with great purpose. He looked so much like King Arthur contemplating Excalibur, I was tempted to kneel before him for possible knighthood. Instead, Peter circled his ersatz sword to the right twice, took a breath through his mouth, blew it out his nose . . . then assumed swing position.

"Golf is not vertical," he told me. "You'd have to stand here [he stepped very close to the ball] to make a vertical golf swing. The circle in golf is almost flat. With tennis or baseball it's a vertical orbit. But in golf we bend over, which puts the circle on an incline.

"Imagine a cart wheel," he continued. "This [he tapped his forearm] is a spoke in the wheel. You're going to be hitting here, on the rim of the wheel. So picture your body as turning in a barrel—the rim of the wheel spins around you. And the main center is right here," he added, tapping his solar plexus, "like in martial arts."

And skiing.

"In a golf swing, the energy comes from the solar plexus, not the arms," Peter went on. "The motor that turns the wheel is in the hips—just a little movement there, and the wheel spins."

Peter gripped the club, raised it swordlike, turned it in another knightly circle, and set the club head behind the ball.

Then he took a swing. Another beautiful shot. About a hundred yards. With a pitching wedge!

"What you want to do is use the natural forces involved. There's the natural force of momentum—once a thing's in motion it wants to keep going. Then there's the natural force of gravity, true gravity—you want to keep good balance at every stage. There's an art to it," he concluded. "When you do it nicely there's no stress on the body. You feel the force, you don't force the feel."

Feel the force? True Gravity. Were Peter Croker and Shivas Irons separated at birth? What was going on here?

"When you force the feel," Peter continued, "it's called 'picking it up,' or 'pulling.' We call that a 'pull.' What we teach is a push. Golf's a push."

He left the practice station and returned with a tennis racket. Then he took a swing with it.

"This is a more visible version of what we do in a golf swing," he explained. "What would you say this racket is doing?"

"It's pushing the air . . . and turning over?"

"Right, so you could say golf is a pushover."

In mid-chortle I remembered something. The shock of it turned an everyday laugh into a sudden banshee-with-the-hiccups imitation. Peter regarded me with raised eyebrows. I regarded him with, I am sure, the wild stare of the recently electrocuted. I grabbed my copy of *Golf in the Kingdom*, excused myself, and ran to the ladies' room.

My memory served me well. Early in Part I, Michael Murphy explains that the name Shivas is derived from the Scottish verb "shive" . . . which means to *push*! And the Scottish word "iron" was not originally a golf club, it was a *sword*. So, the name Shivas Irons actually means "to push the sword," which pretty much summed up Peter's ideal golf swing.

I must have returned to the practice hangar looking like a glazed donut.

"Was it something you ate?" Peter asked delicately.

"No," I said, "it was something I read."

Encouraged, I decided to put some real effort into my practice.

"Feel that?" Peter asked with a nod. "We call that a swing. Doesn't that feel good? You can see the power in that swing. You feel the force. Once you understand the mechanics, you can practice them. But golf is played out there," he said, pointing through the hangar door to the red flag that served as our practice target, "not in here," he said, pointing to his head. "Golf is a balancing act between understanding, which is thinking, and letting go, which is the flow, see. When you're playing your best you're not thinking about it, you're just doing it."

Peter left me that day with two odd new golf rules. One was "Never Try," the other "Expect Nothing."

"To play great golf," he concluded, "you have to be out of your mind—there's just too much other stuff in there."

It definitely was time for my inaugural putting lesson with the inimitable Cindy Swift Jones.

If ever there was a yin-and-yang team, Cindy Jones and Peter Croker were it. Cindy's teaching style was as glittery as Peter's was coiled. Fundamentally, the voltage was the same. While Cindy's motor raced, her eye, like Peter's, missed nothing. Also like her partner's, Cindy's focus remained acute, her information direct and demystifying. Her impeccable professionalism cut through my every false rookie move. I just loved her.

As simple as it was, Cindy's short game lesson was no piece of cake. Utilizing the squaring properties of string and yardsticks, Cindy set up a kind of putter's strike zone that reminded me of my flightmate Tim Arky's golf rule: Memorize the two feet in front and in back of you. Cindy's strike zone included the three feet in front of me, which remained the same even as she backed me farther and farther from the hole.

"Sweep these three feet straight," she assured me, "and you'll be accurate every time."

Presupposing, that is, that one's putting posture is correct. Cindy's concept seemed, well, extreme. She insisted that I was to stand so close to my club and gaze down upon it so directly that it felt more like an Ichabod Crane yoga pose than golf. This was made all the more difficult by Cindy's prescribed putting grip. Thankfully, it was identical to Peter's full-swing grip, but keeping one's left wrist on top of the flat upper plane of a fat putter shaft while hovering over it was torture.

"It hurts," I whined.

"It does at first," Cindy conceded, "but you get used to it."

She ought to know. She won the Wisconsin Women's State Amateur Championship in 1968 and started her apprenticeship in the Professional Golf Association. Then, in 1982, Cindy Swift Jones became the first and only woman to play in the Wisconsin State Open. She shot a 73, too, which was the third-lowest score.

How, I wanted to know, had she become so enamored of this crazy game?

"My father was a golf pro," Cindy replied. "So is my brother. When I was eleven years old a friend and I went out and played fifty-four holes and had a *great* time."

Fifty-four holes?! On her *first* attempt?

"Then, when I was twelve, I won my first tournament. That got my competitive juices going."

So she was a natural. She was also a natural teacher, and lucky for us golf nonnaturals, teaching golf had become Cindy's first love. Champion that she was, she knelt down before me, grasped my putter's club head—which looked to me suspiciously like the head of a dodo bird—and "swept" it.

"A putt is a sweep," Cindy said. "A brush. A pushed brush, *not* a swing."

Then she deftly adjusted my left-palm-heel-on-top grip and made sure my elbows were crooked into a perfect and immovable triangle.

"That triangle doesn't change," Cindy explained. "It just moves back and forth through space, a push. You *never* break your wrist while putting."

Cindy knelt again and placed a yardstick on the putting green in front of me, parallel to my toes, then laid out a straight line of blue string from my ball to the hole. "Stairway to Heaven," I thought.

It didn't matter that I was standing only six inches away— putting straight was the key. The theory was that if you can putt six inches you can putt six feet. Or sixty. The operative word was "straight."

I took my grip, forcing my left hand-heel hard over the top of my putter. I bent my elbows into the appropriate triangle. I practiced my push-sweep stroke. Then, following the blue line, I putted. The ball rolled perfectly and dropped into the hole with that sweet thunk all golfers set their hearts by.

"Tournaments have been lost because pros missed putts that short," Cindy pointed out. "And you understand that seventy percent of your score is your short game."

I did.

She backed me up a few inches, laid down the blue line, and said, "Do it again." I did. The ball dropped in cleanly once again. Regarding me with a clinical eye, she made an almost holographic assessment of my stance and grip. That is, in one hummingbird-quick glance she took in the entire working system. She made a minor adjustment to my shoulders (which tended to rise earward when they were supposed to be relaxed) and slid my left hand-heel painfully back on top of my club. Then she lengthened the blue line once more and backed me farther away from the hole.

"Again."

I practiced my sweeping triangle swing again. Swush. Swush. Then, without warning, something odd happened on about the third one. The motion of the swing shifted from an awkward-feeling imitation to the Real Thing. I felt it. I felt the swing drop into a place of grace. And push through with confidence for the very first time. Cindy, of course, knew before I did.

"That's IT!" she all but cried. "That's the putting stroke."

Like every other golf rookie in the known universe, my next thought was a train wreck. "What if I can't do it again!?" As soon as I thought it, I couldn't. Cindy immediately stepped into my strike zone, and like Peter before her, grasped the shaft of the putter and pulled it through in perfect swing form.

There was no ego in the teaching styles of Peter Croker and Cindy Jones, no posturing, no showing off to us mere neophytes. They put their perceptual genius directly in the service of their students. I needed to sincerely thank Graham for this gift.

I continued my triangular sweep and Cindy continued to back me away from my target. The three-foot blue line remained the same. The farther away I stood, the more I missed the hole, given the compounded difficulties of putting speed and green aberrations. But I also made an unnatural percentage of putts, especially at the longer distances. It was, I knew, dependent on memorizing both the feeling of a proper putt-push and those First Three Feet. Straight and true, over and over and over. If I hadn't already mastered (well, almost) fly casting with ten thousand casts I wouldn't have understood the magic of repetition. Or the importance of it.

I also already knew that I loved putting. Maybe it *was* all that miniature golf. Maybe putting just felt less out-of-control. But I knew I liked the delicacy of it, like casting a hand-tied fly with a flexing 5-weight, compared with heaving a giant fly into the blue with a telephone pole of a saltwater fishing rod.

Leaning far over my putter, I triangulated away in that smarting South Carolina light. A white egret strutted comically around the far end of a nearby pond while swallows looped along the surface of the water, leaving elusive trails in my peripheral vision. Once a shockingly heavy-bodied bumblebee buzzed by with great importance. "Stay the course," it seemed to say. Slowly, my putting became straighter and more accurate. It was at the very least encouraging, at best a little eerie.

So focused was I on my putting practice that I hadn't noticed Cindy's disappearance. She had, it turned out, only visited the ladies' room, but when I looked around to find her I found instead a crow. It stood bright black on the edge of the green to my right, maybe five feet away, glittering with intelligence, its head cocked as if in amusement. I had no idea how long it had been there, but I had the strange sense that once Cindy left, it had taken over, directing, as it were, from the wings. Before I could edit myself I said out loud:

"Graham?"

9

miss bell driving

There was a phone message from Graham when I returned to my hotel that evening. He had arranged for me to meet two local women golfers before I flew off to North Carolina to see Peggy Kirk Bell, one of the most legendary women golfers in America.

On Hilton Head, Ethel Hunter is a woman golf legend in her own right. As promised, I found her on the practice putting green of the island's National Golf Course. Tiny and trim, she was so focused on her putting I was loath to interrupt, and stood, instead, watching her make one spectacular putt after another. It took two seconds to figure out Graham's intention: Practice like Ethel does and you, too, can putt like a pro at age ninety-three.

Ethel, it turned out, had begun her sporting life as a Vassar tennis player.

"But I like to be outdoors," she explained in a voice as sweet and southern as angel food cake. "And in golf you don't have to have a partner. I used to grab a caddie named Tadpole and just go."

"Just going" appeared to be a trademark of Ethel's, because on that note she turned on her golf spikes and walked away.

"Ethel!" I called after her. "Do you have any advice for a novice woman golfer?"

She turned back so swiftly I thought I had offended her. Her soft southern ways lifted like a ball gown in the wind, revealing a surprising amount of muscle underneath. She fixed me with one of the most no-nonsense stares I've ever been on the receiving end of, and in a tone that bordered on the imperious said: **"Keep your damn head down."**

From the looks of her home it was hard to believe that Cherry Gillespie was a golfer. She and her husband, Bill, were golf pals of Graham's, and he had left me directions to a neighboring island where they had their summer place. I stepped inside and became catatonic—it was like stepping *into* a Matisse painting. Great planes of color filled every wall, vivid, graphic, and utterly elegant. Almost no one knows how to use color like that. The furnishings and art were perfect, too. And every single decor decision had been Cherry's. She was, I had no doubt, an interior design genius.

I was so taken by the place I almost forgot I'd come to talk golf. (All I wanted to do was talk *color*!) But Cherry is as passionate a golfer as she is a designer, and soon we were standing on the Gillespies' country club course, where she cut quite a figure with her Nordic face and thick blond hair. Surely when Cherry was twenty she could have passed for a film star. She probably could today.

The Gillespies tried to persuade me to play a round with them, but I demurred, publicly citing a lack of readiness while privately guarding a desire to stay healthy. The Gillespies were serious golfers, and I knew full well that after two holes somebody would shoot me. I did, however, agree to walk with them as they played. I said I'd take notes. It would be, I told Cherry, the first time I'd watched a serious woman golfer play golf.

"Now I want you to see this," Cherry began. "This is the women's tee—they moved it and didn't bother to replace the markers."

It was clear that "they" would hear about the faux pas. Cherry teed up and addressed the ball. She performed, I noted, a preswing ritual almost identical to Peter Croker's Excalibur Routine. Then she took a swing. It was a thing of beauty, a flawless semiarc executed with both power and grace. Her ball, needless to say, soared. So did Bill's. "How nice," I thought, "for one excellent golfer to be married to another." Cherry agreed.

"But it's great to play golf by yourself sometimes," she added. "A little private time."

She found her drive off the 4th tee less than satisfactory.

"It's a tight lie," she explained. "I should have played off the middle of my stance—that's with a wood."

She followed, however, with a Pro-Am 50-foot putt.

Her drive off the 5th tee was fantastic. Cherry neither smiled nor said anything, then pronounced her husband's even better drive "surgical."

"Luke, Chapter 7, Verse 16," replied Bill. Perhaps he meant he thought he'd hit at only 80 percent. Or maybe he chalked his fine playing up to knowing the course so well, the proverbial Prodigal Son. Considering Cherry, I went a little further: No one can serve two masters; I was convinced that in her world, art and golf are one.

Her second shot hit a bunker on the right and put the fear of God in her. Cherry overcompensated and ended up on the green, well left of the pin.

"See, that's a mental mistake," she told me. "That sand trap shouldn't be thought of as bad. It should be thought of as friendly. You get in—who cares, you get out. All good, all good. Everything on a golf course is all good."

Her putt was short.

"They watered it!" she cried. "Jesus, Bill, this is water!"

For practice, she took the putt again . . . and sank it.

Bill laughed. "Graham told me what Sam Snead told him when he did that."

"What?" Cherry asked.

" 'A mule could do it the second time.' "

Cherry was not amused. But she rallied.

"A great marriage in vitro," I thought. That Kodak Moment was diminished a second later when Cherry pointed to a dark shape in the green water to our right.

"Alligator," she declared.

Yikes.

During the remainder of the game Cherry also pointed out live oaks, water oaks, and loblolly pine, a red cardinal, and even an anhinga, or "snake bird." We also saw an osprey run a bald eagle off his moss-bearded nest while sounding the high-pitched alarm I'd heard osprey make so many times back home in Oregon on my beloved McKenzie River. Ethel Hunter was right: If you like the outdoors, you'll like golf.

The game ended in a cliff-hanger—literally. Cherry's fine final putt came to a rest on the edge of the cup. It was the only time I'd seen her near anger.

"Every hit in golf makes somebody happy," Bill offered.

"And if I'd overhit it ten feet it would still count the same," Cherry said miserably.

"Yes," Bill agreed with only the slightest hint of triumph. "Golf is not like horseshoes."

"Now, this traffic circle is *bad*," Peggy Kirk Bell announced suddenly.

At least that's what I thought she said. It was hard to hear over the engine of her car, which sounded a lot like a blenderful of golf balls. We were, after all, driving around in her vintage London taxi, which she had graciously asked her mechanic to revive so we could go to town in style.

I had left the Gillespies for a quick flight to Pinehurst, North Carolina. A polite young valet named Joe met me at the tiny Moore County Airport. "Oh, you've never met anyone like Peggy," he said when I asked what it was like to work for her. "She could be up on the roof sweeping off pine needles when you get there." Fortunately, she was finishing lunch and in the mood to show me the golf-mad town of Pinehurst, America's original golf capital.

"People don't know how to drive it," Peggy continued, sizing up the infinite dogleg left of this Romanesque intersection with a golf pro's intensity. "They stay out in the right lane the whole time. But if they stay in, then they can cut over and go where they want to go. See, this is the way you're supposed to drive it. I'm going in."

I fought the urge to duck and cover. Toyotas and Volvos skittered in all directions. A FedEx truck ran for its life. All drivers within a 360-degree radius offered gestures and facial expressions uncommon to normal southern hospitality, and all were directed at *me*, since I occupied the British passenger seat, the usual driver's seat in America. I considered pointing to Peggy in self-defense, but it was soon clear that you don't need to draw attention to the last living legend of American women's golf in the Golf Mecca of America. This was Pinehurst, North Carolina. This was Peggy Kirk Bell, and this was her town.

Miss Bell, as locals call her, owns two of Pinehurst's most revered golf resorts, Pine Needles Lodge & Golf Club and, across the street, the elegant Mid Pines Inn & Golf Club. With Peggy, as she prefers to be called, serving as honorary chairman, Pine Needles hosted the 1996 U.S. Women's Open Championship and will host it again in the year 2001, a fitting triumph for a founding member of the Ladies Professional Golf Association with one of the finest records in women's golf.

Given her schedule, to this day I don't know how Graham managed to persuade Peggy to meet with me.

A native of Findlay, Ohio, Peggy was a three-time winner of the Ohio Women's Amateur Championship. In 1947, her peer and friend Babe Zaharias asked her to be her partner in the International Four Ball Championship, played in Hollywood, Florida. They won it, eliminating Louise Suggs and Jean Hopkins in the finals. "No, Babe won it," Peggy insists. "I just helped a little."

In 1949, Peggy took Pinehurst's famed North and South Amateur, as well as the Augusta Titleholders Championship, where she broke by a shot the tournament record of 300 for seventy-two holes. The following year she made the Curtis Cup team, then won the 1950 Eastern Amateurs Championship and finally turned pro with A. G. Spaulding, the company she represents to this day. In 1953, Peggy and her late husband, Warren "Bullet" Bell, purchased Pine Needles, which is halfway between the towns of Pinehurst and Southern Pines, and then settled into an admirable, thoroughly golf-centered life, raising two daughters and a son, all of whom are now active in the management of the family resorts.

At seventy-seven, Peggy still looked like a pro golfer—the tan, the signature white visor, the spikeless Spaulding teaching shoes. She was wonderfully lean and had the easy carriage of an athletic woman a third her age. The only signs of her approaching octogenarianism were sun lines, a hearing aid she refuses to wear, and a bandage on the back of her left hand telegraphing recent skin cancer surgery.

Surprisingly accessible for a divot diva, Peggy Kirk Bell remains the soul of Pine Needles, its definite box office draw. Acting as a sort of mercurial overseer, she swoops unannounced through the dining room, club room, and bar, chatting with thrilled guests and giving semidictatorial orders to the nearest employee about the finer points of service and housekeeping.

It was a good day for a drive. On every street, great bonnets of pink azaleas underscored dogwood trees in full white bloom. Pine trees were everywhere; a cinnamon-colored thatch of pine needles covered almost all open ground. Botanical beauty aside, the South was still being tortured by tornado weather. I eyed the black-bellied thunderheads above us. Peggy dismissed them with a glance. "They're already by us," she said in a voice so sure it made you feel safe from all possible calamity, despite the alarm our London taxi continued to evoke from fellow drivers. The underpowered, oversized vehicle lurched along, perilously close to other objects, moving and non. Privately, I suspected vision problems. But Peggy never hit a thing. In fact, she cleanly missed all obstacles by the microinch; to Miss Bell this was just another precisely timed long drive.

"We're heading west toward Pinehurst," she said. "There are forty-some golf courses within five miles of here. That's a little par-3 course there. There's another—Talamore Golf Course; they have llamas to carry your golf bags. There's the Plantation—an Arnold Palmer course. Here's Midland Country Club on the right. Now on our left is the National—that was built by Jack Nicklaus. I used to play there. I belong to the Country Club of North Carolina, too, which is where a lot of locals play.

"Okay," she said, nodding to the fairway on our left, "this is Pinehurst Number Two, the most famous golf course in the country. Maybe in the world. They had the Men's Open here in '99. Let's go in."

Peggy brought the taxi to a jolting halt right in front. Everything from the hotel itself to smaller buildings was whitewashed and trimmed in hunter green, Pinehurst's traditional colors. Most sported dark green awnings as well. Valets and waiting caddies nodded their respect as we walked. "Hello, Miss Bells" rang out like Hail Marys. Even a black-faced fox squirrel on a nearby tree trunk chattered out a welcome. Peggy greeted everyone, then shouldered her way through the front door and strode purposefully down a long entry hall decorated with golf awards on the right, display cases filled with golf mementos on the left.

"Here's where we used to eat," she announced, motioning to a cavernous glassed-in dining room. "Now it's the Donald Ross Grill Room. That's Billy Joe Patton," she said, staring at a black-and-white wall photo. "He should have won the Masters. Finished third. Blew it on the last stroke. And there's Babe, Patty Berg, Snead, Arnie, Byron, Jack, Hogan, Player, Francis." Peggy repeated the litany of golf greats like she was calling family members for dinner.

"There's you!" I said, perhaps too enthusiastically. An entire glass case was devoted to Peggy Kirk Bell memorabilia. Peggy smiled.

"There's my book," she said, eyeing a 1950 copy of *A Woman's Way to Better Golf*. "And there's Babe and me." They were posed on the cover of the April-May 1947 issue of *The Woman Golfer* magazine. "There's my plane."

"You're a pilot, too?"

"Oh, yeah. A girlfriend from California and I were playing a tournament in the early days and got stuck in an airport in Texas. And she told me, 'Peggy, if you buy a plane I'll teach you to fly.' So we found a plane for eight thousand dollars and I wrote a check and called my father so he'd cover it. Then we flew it back to California. I stayed there and took flying lessons until I soloed, then I flew it home to Ohio."

A silver-haired man stopped us in the hall.

"Peggy Kirk Bell?" he asked.

"Yeah," Peggy replied.

"Wow," he breathed.

He then gestured royally to Peggy, and declared to no one in particular: "This is golf history."

"I AM history," Peggy said, laughing. "Let's go."

"Are you in the Golf Hall of Fame?" I yelled to Peggy over the grinding taxi engine.

"No," she replied flatly. "I'm in the North Carolina Hall of

Fame, and the Ohio Hall of Fame, but to be in the LPGA Hall of Fame you have to have won thirty-some tournaments. It's the dumbest thing in the world. They've only got thirteen people in it and nobody's gonna be able to win that many tournaments anymore. They're gonna have to change it . . . Okay, now we're in the town of Pinehurst."

Peggy angled the taxi down a charming little street of post-colonial brick buildings dating from the late 1800s.

"Look down the alleyways and you'll see all these little shops, sort of like Carmel, only a lot older. That big building used to be our theater. I'm old enough to remember when men wore tuxes and women wore formals to go to the movies! Okay," she proclaimed suddenly, "I'm taking you to the Country Club."

The inner rooms of the Country Club of North Carolina carry the sacrosanct atmosphere of all architectural tributes to southern society. Peggy blasted right through it like Harrison Ford in the *Temple of Doom,* "Hello, Miss Bells" following her like benedictions.

"The Masters on?" she replied.

It soon was, and we were offered a finely set table in front of the television. Except for the highly cordial staff, we had the room to ourselves. We ordered tea. Some kind of excellent southern pecan cookies arrived with it. Peggy asked for peanuts, and a bowl of jumbo red-skinned Georgia specials appeared.

"Freddie Couples is four under par," said the TV commentator.

"Well, he'll make that," Peggy said right back.

"He's in second place," the TV added.

"Looks like Watson," Peggy replied. "They all have the same cap nowadays. Oh, I want to see that cute one. Is he playing with Tiger today? I tell you, I can't see anymore. Could you turn the volume up a bit? My hearing aid went out and I took it off. There's Freddie. What hole's he on?"

"I think the seventh or eighth," a handsome waiter answered, clearly pleased to be of golf service.

"Did he start on one or the back?"

"He started on one."

"He's not gonna make it around," Peggy warned. "Would you like some of these nuts? They're not the big ones." Peggy had peeled every one she ate. A hillock of red skins grew beside her teacup like some kind of strange southern insect hatch.

"Scott McCarron at the twelfth," said the TV. "And that's the fifth ball into the water today."

Atlanta was still suffering from fierce storm winds.

"I like him," Peggy declared. "Nice boy."

"Have you met Tiger yet?" I asked.

"Um-hmm. He's great. He's gonna be around a long time, that Tiger. He said that his mother is responsible for his concentration. She's Thai."

"I didn't know that," I replied. "Wow, so she's Buddhist."

"Hence the inner calm," I thought.

"Who taught you to play golf?" I asked Peggy.

"Oh, well, I think the Lord just directed my life. I was seventeen and very upset that I was too old to go to summer camp. That night my dad came home and said, 'If any of you youngsters want to go out and play golf, we belong to the country club now.' And I thought, 'Well, I'll go learn to play golf this summer.' So I went down to my dad's warehouse—he had a wholesale grocery business—and they had a big athletic room and I got this little bag with a three-wood, a three-iron, a five, seven, nine, a putter, and three balls. So I go. I had a '28 Oakland Roadster—paid fifty-seven dollars for it—and I went out there and said, 'Where do you start?' And the guy told me, 'Right there.' So, I went over and put my ball down and hit it . . . into the woods. I went in to look for it and couldn't find it. I hit another one . . . back in the woods.

Hit another one. I was an hour on the first tee trying to find my three balls. So, I walked into the golf shop and said, 'Who's the teacher here?' And the guy said, 'I am.' And I said, 'Well, how do you hold it?'—I was holding it just like a baseball bat. And he said, 'Do you want a lesson?' And I said, 'Yes.' And he said, 'Tomorrow morning, nine o'clock.' I was there by eight. Lessons were fifty cents. It was during the Depression. You could get a chicken dinner for thirty-five cents—salad, pie, the whole thing. Well, I played every day until dark—loved it. Just got hooked because I couldn't do it . . . Hey, there's Duval with a birdie. He's awful good. I wish he'd shave. Who'd they say is gonna make it?"

"John Daly," the handsome waiter answered. "He's plus four, I believe."

"Plus four'll make it? How's Montgomery? Show it," she ordered the TV. "Even."

Fred Couples appeared.

"See how he stops at the top? He has great timing. His change of direction is great. You want this cookie? Go ahead, I'm not going to eat it. I'm not gonna eat any more peanuts, either."

"Again, today is cut day," the TV announced. "The top forty-four and ties or any player within ten shots of the lead will qualify for the weekend. We have a three-way tie: Tiger Woods in defense of his Masters title, with Scott Hoch and '92 champion Fred Couples."

"Scott Hoch's mother came to my golf school twice," Peggy said. "She's good. That didn't look like Azinger," she told the TV. "He's a good boy. I love him, *love* him. Zinger came and played at our Cheap Shot Tournament at Pine Needles. He hadn't won a thing. The guy he played with was a Chevrolet dealer, and he sold him a car real cheap. Zinger left with his first car."

"Jack Nicklaus goes to two under par!" the TV cried.

"Jack never quits," Peggy replied softly. "I'd never count him out. He wouldn't be there if he didn't think he could win. Is his son with him?"

"Yes," the waiter told her. "He's on his cell phone."

"Which son?"

"Gary, I believe."

"Jack Jr.'s the one who was with him when he won it. [Duval appears again and tees off.] I like his golf swing, Duval's," Peggy said approvingly. "I just don't like his whiskers."

"More tea, ladies?" asked an elegantly dressed woman who seemed to be in charge.

"No thanks," Peggy replied. "Okay. Let's go. We're outta here. Thank you, gang! Let's hit the ladies' room," she whispered as we left. "All that tea."

As we washed our hands, I glanced in the mirror and was shocked to see the age difference on our faces. Though more than twice my age, Peggy Kirk Bell has the I'll-try-anything spirit of my youngest pals. I now knew why virtually everyone in pro golf loves her. And why the walls at Pine Needles are alive with old black-and-white photos of beskirted young women golfers—America's best, in their prime—all smiling, all posing with Peggy, who surely was the best golfing girl-friend a girl could have.

"Come on," she said. "I want to get back before it's dark so I can see your golf swing. Now, let's pray that the taxi starts."

It did, of course.

Back at Pine Needles, Peggy grabbed a bag of clubs, swung them on her back, and walked me down to the driving range.

I was unbearably nervous. Peggy noticed my hands, still tattooed with Peter Croker's swing position markings.

"You've seen Peter," she said. She didn't say that she had seen him herself the year before. Golf pros, apparently, are as proud as master fishing coaches, who will always regard flies tied by someone else with dull interest, then silently tie on one of their own.

"I'm nervous," I told Peggy.

"Aw, it's just golf," she said back. "Look, it's like this."

She teed up and took the most beautiful, perfectly relaxed golf swing imaginable. As smooth as Peter's. As graceful as Cherry's. But with an indefinable cool that is all her own and remains, even now, Peggy Kirk Bell's trademark. Her ball made that jet-taking-off sound, and, indeed, took off into the menacing North Carolina sky.

"Now, you do it," she said.

Somehow, Peggy made it look so unrushed, so almost unimportant, that I just walked up to the ball and hit it. Just like that. It flew an amazing 150 yards. Even Peggy was impressed.

"You know," she said, patting me on the back, "I think you're gonna be one of those little girls who hits it a mile."

10

....

saint nancy
and the golf corset

When a genuine woman golf legend voluntarily tells you you
have genuine golf potential, you believe her. Between Peter
Croker's and Cindy Jones's stalwart teaching and Peggy's final
benediction, I walked in my front door a changed . . . golfer.
No longer did I secretly consider myself an impostor, a faux
player whose pause at the top of her backswing was even a faux
pause. No more would my mind scream "Train Wreck!" whenever I accelerated toward contact—it would, instead, whisper
"Expect Nothing." I knew, finally, that I was done with the notion that the grand old game was simply beyond the likes of
me. In short, the game had ceased to be a royal pain in the
neck and, instead, had been transformed into a regal quest.

I *would* be a golfer.

Say amen, somebody.

Somebody did. Because waiting for me in my living room
when I returned from the mid-Atlantic coast was my own Excalibur.

At first I thought it was a lamp.

"I don't remember ordering that," I said out loud, but the
box was clearly addressed to me. I called the manager of the
building, who informed me that the box was so big and

looked so important she'd gone ahead and put it in my apartment for me while I was gone.

There was no mistaking it—the thing in the box was mine. The most unnerving part was the return address: *Nancy Lopez Golf.* Nancy Lopez!!? Golf??! If Peggy Kirk Bell is the Queen Mother of American Golf, then Nancy Lopez is the Queen. Somehow, the Golf Queen had seen fit to make contact with one of her lowliest subjects.

How could this be?

And so it was with melodramatic angst that I undid the sacred seals of the Nancy Lopez Box . . . with the help of a pair of way-dull scissors and, finally, out of extreme frustration, a Cuisinart blade held, ceremoniously, in my golf-gloved hand. If I were to shed blood over the Queen's Gift, so be it.

What was inside that would have been worth shedding blood over? GOLF CLUBS!

My very own set of golf clubs! In their very own loden-green golf bag that just *happened* to go perfectly with my hair.

But these weren't just any golf clubs. Oh, no. These were *Nancy Lopez Golf Clubs*! Nancy Lopez Golf Clubs? Impossible! There are no Nancy Lopez Golf Clubs. There are no *women's* golf clubs. Women golfers, like women fly fisherpersons, have had to limp along with too-big grips and too-stiff shafts and too-big wading boots and too-long-in-the-torso/too-short-in-the-leg waders that give women anglers an unbecoming melting sausage appearance. This is because the grand old sports of both golf and fly fishing have been dominated, nay, *defined* by men.

Suspecting a marketing hoax, I read the tag warily. The first words on it were:

DEBUT '98

NANCY**LOPEZ**GOLF
Defining the Women's Game

"They probably just bought the rights to her name," I scoffed. Smart move. Everyone knows women are pouring into the game. With larceny in my heart, I read the inside of the folded tag:

OUR PHILOSOPHY

NancyLopezGolf is dedicated to
Defining the Women's Game
through leading products and activities
that enhance the complete golf
experience for women.

The complete golf experience for women? This sounded serious.

Was it true? Was Nancy Lopez, the *real* Nancy Lopez, making golf clubs for *us*? And golf bags, complete with a double-entry ball pocket (for when you forget to aim your bag cart in the right direction when you park it), a zippered rain hood (especially handy if you happen to live in Clam Weather Central like I do), really cool Nancy Lopez headcovers for each wood, a neat ring for attaching my Nancy Lopez golf glove and Nancy Lopez towel, both of which were included in my mysterious care package, and best of all: a purse! Well, the brochure called it a "removable satchel," but it was big enough for a woman's golf essentials, such as lipstick, comb, sunblock, credit card, sunglasses, car keys, and sanitary you-know-whats . . . which solved the vexing problem of how to carry all that stuff while you're on the golf course. (I had tried to stash an actual purse in my golf bag when I played Toka-tee with Graham, and the strap kept getting so tangled in the bag cart wheels that I finally had to *wear* the thing . . . kind of a "Jackie O. Goes Golfing" look.)

My golf bag, I noted, was called a "Roscoe Bag" after Nancy's first LPGA Tour caddie, Kim "Roscoe" Jones, who had helped her win the first twenty-eight of her nearly fifty titles. There was even a handsome visor in that magical box—crow-black, I noted, with "Nancy Lopez" embroidered in white on the brim. I loved it.

But the clubs were the thing that must have captured the conscience of the Queen. First of all, they were beautiful. Second, they felt *right*. It's hard to explain, but the feeling reminded me of the first time I held my Joan Wulff Favorite Winston trout rod, with its mercifully indented grip. The small bones of your hand just seem to sit down and make their dainty selves at home with a rare kind of comfort guys just can't understand, having had every piece of sports gear in their entire lives designed just for them.

In seconds I was up on the roof deck swinging away in the rain. Rookie that I was, the beauty of Nancy's clubs-in-action was not lost on me; they were perfect. They felt so *light*, so *balanced*. The best of new technology had been worked deeply into their design—for me, a *woman*. They were also perfect because they were *mine*.

I didn't actually know why they were mine, but I had a pretty good idea: Graham, again. He seemed to know everyone who was anyone in golf. An even bigger mystery was this: By what miracle had Nancy Lopez decided to launch her new company, the first golf company ever founded and owned by a woman, right when I was taking up golf? Besides generic gratitude, it was impossible not to feel a kinship with her. By virtue of pure cosmic coincidence, Nancy Lopez became, at that moment, my own personal golf saint. I placed her "Roscoe Bag" tag on my home altar, and to this day say a little golf prayer to it every time I leave for the golf course. And I say one to her. Because I sensed without a sand trap of a doubt that Nancy Lopez has a heart as wide as the world's worst slice and as long as its longest drive. If ever I was granted the grace to meet the woman in person, I vowed, I'd thank her for caring enough about all the struggling girl duffers on the planet, and the five million American women golfers in general, to build us a set of clubs that don't feel like damn Louisville Sluggers in our kitchen-weary, laundry-tired, wife-mother-daughter-grandmother, Just-do-it, twenty-first-century hands.

the golf corset

Once a woman has her own set of brand-new golf clubs, her old golf outfits start to look pretty shabby. The truth be known, women's golf clothes were problematic for me from the beginning.

First of all, they're not women's golf clothes, they're men's. Men look great in golf shirts and pleated khaki slacks. On a woman, unless she is uncommonly tall and narrow, standard golf clothes look frumpy.

The reasons are obvious. Golf shirts were designed for someone with big shoulders, no bust, and no waist—i.e., A Guy. Put one on a woman and you've got a bag lady. The shirt's sleeves are floppy and far too wide, its seams lie haplessly on a woman's upper arms fully inches down from her shoulders, and a bodice of loose fabric falls unappealingly free from the tip of even a modest chest. Definitely your basic Bag Lady Look above board.

Pleated khaki slacks below board don't help. They were invented for someone with narrow hips. Show me a woman with narrow hips and I'll show you either a teenager or 1 percent of the general adult female population. If you've ever taken an anatomy class, you'll know this is true. The way you tell a male skeletal pelvis from a female is the width of its ilium, those flared elephant-ear bones that jut out many inches wider in women than in men. Add muscle on top of that and even a minimum of female fat and the last thing you need is pleats.

If you don't believe me, look at a J. Crew catalogue. The models are close to six feet tall, naturally narrow-hipped, and unnaturally lean, even compared with those of us who work out and eat right. BUT . . . compare how they look in something form-fitting—cigarette pants, Capris, a slim short skirt, classic jeans—with how they look in a pair of pleated khakis: whammo! Their boyish hips are suddenly six inches wider and they don't seem so tall and willowy anymore, which speaks volumes for the rest of us, *literally*. So, between guy golf shirts and guy pleated slacks, golf clothes are not a woman golfer's best friend.

This is not surprising. The history of both women's sports and women's outdoor wear has been a slow climb out of man's brain, which, for a good twenty-five hundred years, was convinced that women were frail, brainless possessions suited only to the delicate acts of childbirth and baking nine loaves of bread a day. With, of course, the exception of upper-class women, who were merely expected to direct servants, faint often, and somehow manage to produce heirs. Fainting was easy—from the sixteenth through the early twentieth centuries women couldn't breathe. It had everything to do with the nature of general feminine attire: From the 1500s until about 1920, women were held captive in the bone-and-iron jaws of corsets no matter *what* they were doing.

The earliest corsets were made of boiled leather or tightly laced heavy canvas fitted with wooden stays. During the Renaissance, wire and steel were substituted, and after 1600 the English introduced whalebone, which, despite untold misfortune for whales, at least flexed a little.

Real relief finally arrived in the late 1700s, when Paris decided to copy the old Greek- and Roman-style loose-fitting chemise. Unhappily, that breath of fresh air only lasted a few decades; by 1830 an eighteen-inch waist once again had become the ideal. The steel corset was back with a vengeance, and remained in place until women won the vote.

Thus, for hundreds of years, women's bodies were not only extraordinarily constricted, they were utterly concealed, both of which made sports out of the question. Of course, women weren't allowed to play them anyway.

Until the end of the 1800s, the one sport available to even privileged women was horseback riding (and that was only because of the influence of Napoleon's wife, Empress Eugenie de Montijo de Guzmán, a passionate Spanish horsewoman). But by the late 1890s it was, for the first time, fashionable for society women to be active, despite the fact that peasant women had been nothing but that forever, though you can hardly call taking in the wheat "sport." Well-to-do women, by then, had gone mad for bicycles, and both men and women did their cycling in knickers, whose ancestors were bloomers and whose descendants, ironically enough, were golf knickers.

Tennis came next, and with it the navy serge skirt, a mannish shirt, and a sailor hat. Archery soon brought waves of feminine contestants who competed in wide trousers. In England women even took up cricket, and soon after . . . **Golf!** . . . finally golf, which they played in skirts, coats, ankle boots, and jaunty hats, like their Scottish role models, who were the first women golfers on earth.

These early female golfers had to contend with that serious fashion challenge: the corset. In her beautiful book *One Hundred Years of Women's Golf,* author Lewine Mair confirms the existence of the golf corset. ". . . The average woman golfer," she reports, "was by all accounts encased in corsets replete with whale bones and lacing."

Not only were Scottish women golfers beholden to the Victorian style, they were obliged, on a near-daily basis, to endure Scotland's famous inclement weather. Mair cites one case that occurred during what she calls "the English championship of 1924 at Cooden Beach in the Pevensey Marshes," where a contestant's knitted wool skirt became so saturated with rain that she couldn't move and asked special permission to "repair to the clubhouse" and change her skirt, or at least wring the thing out. "Though there was no known precedent," writes Mair, "the LGU [Ladies' Golf Union] gave their blessing to the donning of a new skirt." Beginning fresh and unfettered on the 18th hole, the woman won the tournament.

Thank goodness I didn't have the golf garb problems of my predecessors. But the basic challenge was the same: I wanted to be comfortable *and* look good. So was the challenge of my usual golfing weather, Oregon being a slightly greener and wetter version of Scotland. Thus did I recruit my long-term fashion consultant and sports buddy, Lauri Doyle, a passionate soccer player with great refined taste, who happened to fly in from California to visit me just after my Nancy Lopez Golf Clubs arrived.

"We just wear shorts and jerseys," she offered a little discompassionately.

"Yeah, well, you run all over the place in soccer," I replied. "Golf is . . . more *respectable*."

"Or just slower," Lauri replied coolly. "So, what do most women golfers wear?"

"Golf shirts and pleated slacks."

"Oh. That is a problem," Lauri agreed. She might be a soccer fanatic, but she had her style limits. There was nothing left to do but go golf clothes shopping.

"What does this Graham guy wear to play golf?" my friend asked on the way to the mall.

"Golf shirts and pleated slacks. Of course, he looks great in them."

"Uh-huh." She was starting to see my dilemma.

"So how did you meet him, anyway?"

I told her the whole story and winced while awaiting her response.

"So, he just shows up on golf courses? And sets up all these golf things for you and leaves strange things on your doorstep, but won't take you out in public because his divorce isn't final?"

I nodded. She sounded just like Rande. Why do your girlfriends always make guys sound worse than you think they are?

"Jess, he's a control freak."

At least that was better than a golf stalker. Wasn't it?

"So," my pal of twenty-five years concluded, "are you going to let this guy have everything on his terms?"

I hadn't thought of it in those terms.

"Well," I answered in a voice that sounded the way a dog with its tail between its legs looks, "he said he'd look for us tonight at Riverdance."

Lauri rolled her eyes. Luckily, we had arrived at the mall.

Our destination was one of those cavernous multistory, all-inclusive sporting stores that sell every kind of athletic clothing and equipment. We walked past rows of sporty shoes, racks of aerobics leotards and biking shorts, various styles of helmets, an entire section of home workout machines and free weights. There were baseball, football, basketball, and, yes, soccer stations (Lauri looked wistfully, but dutifully refrained from stopping). Handsome vertical pictures of Nike athletes hung from the ceiling in every direction like homages to royalty. Finally we came to golf.

Four-fifths of the golf department was taken up by golf clubs and men's golf clothes. Only two circular racks and a couple of tables were devoted to women's golf clothes, and most of the items offered were in colors better suited to swimsuits and Popsicles. They didn't even have Nancy Lopez clubs yet.

"See," I said, "it's pathetic."

"No kidding," Lauri commiserated.

"The only golf clothes I really like are Ralph Lauren's," I said.

My fashionable friend brightened.

"Ralph Lauren makes golf clothes?!"

"Sort of. Not many. Not enough, anyway."

As usual, there was one small Ralph Lauren rack. In truth, Ralph's styles weren't all that much better than the usual guy-girl golf clothes, but the colors and quality were. The shirts, while belabored with the usual three-button placket, unflattering short sleeves, and dippy Peter Pan collar, were, at least, cut for women and came in true women's sizes. And their colors had adult integrity: white, a rich indigo, cocoa, and a dusty sage I coveted. The slacks, as always, were beautifully tailored though they all had those damn pleats. Better yet were the golf shoes.

"Ralph Lauren makes *golf* shoes?" Lauri said.

"Amazing, isn't it."

O, they were beautiful. Modified wing tips replete with careful constellations of microholing as handsomely patterned as a trout's back. They were, of course, once again knockoffs of men's shoes, but at least they were classic, because the other problem with women's golf clothes is what appears to be an obsession with kitsch.

Women's golf sweaters, for instance, generally tend toward the florid, as if somehow turning shapeless planes of cheap acrylic knit into watercolor canvases converts these forms from waistless to "womanly." Women's golf shirts retain that untenable polo shirt style which makes for especially lethal collisions when paired with such "feminine" colors as Grandma Lilac or Little Girl Hot Pink. Pleated golf slacks, as we already know, are pleated golf slacks. But the worst are women's golf jackets. For some reason their designers have it in their heads to turn golf jackets into billowing odes to faux riveting, outdoor scenes inexplicably filled with hunting dogs and mountains, giant roses, little-kid drawings, and random sprays of rhinestones that, to my eye, say "Nashville," not "St Andrews."

So a nice, simple pair of women's white wing-tip golf

shoes were a joy to behold. Their price tag, however, was not. The dang things cost close to $200. And my beloved sage-green golf shirt was almost $100.

Lauri and I were so put off by the prices that we migrated to the lone sale rack and found two acceptable golf shirts in my size, one in white, one in navy, both form-fitting (though not tight) and long-sleeved, a style element that banishes forever the sloppy flop of guy-golf-shirt-arm. Also, long sleeves remain ideal for most of Oregon's golf weather, which more often than not requires an unobtrusive golf sweater. I have a one-word answer to that article of golf clothing: cropped. A cropped light wool or cotton sweater offers the needed upper-body warmth but by hitting a woman at her waist, not her hips, *gives* her a waist, doesn't emphasize her hips, and doesn't have loose folds to get in the way of even chip shots.

As for the rest of my golf ensemble, I've come to resoundingly agree with Lady Joyce Heathcoat-Amory, winner, from 1922 to 1929, of four British Amateur Championships. "Trousers apart," she concluded after her visit to Hilton Head to watch the Women's Masters, "the only practical garment has to be a short skirt such as the Americans now wear."

The concept of the short golf skirt brings up a most interesting question. My beloved nongolfing, culturally astute novelist friend, Valerie Brooks, put it this way:

"What I'd like to know is if the Scottish invented golf, why in the world don't they play in *kilts*?"

11

go see al

"That's him!" I whispered to Lauri.

"Where?"

"Up there!"

I had spotted Graham in the balcony on the other side of the auditorium. It was as close to a real date as we'd had. Nonetheless, we'd managed to play golf together every three days or so for weeks. And like the simmering courtships of old, the enforced restraint had intensified our mutual attraction to unbearable levels.

Lauri followed my gaga-gaze heavenward, then blinked.

"He's with a *woman*!" she whispered.

"That's his sister."

Lauri shook her head.

"His *sister*," she hissed. "Why didn't he take *you* to this thing?"

"I *told* you . . . the divorce."

"Whatta wimp," Lauri declared.

"But he's cute, don't you think?"

"I can't *see* him from here," Lauri replied. Then she added, "Ted Bundy was cute," and made the same face Rande had when I told her about the We-can't-be-seen-in-public mandate. Already my two longest-term best friends didn't like Graham, and they hadn't even met him yet.

Neither the exuberance of Irish music nor the passion of Riverdance could take my mind off Graham. I at least should have been thinking about golf. The exquisite way Riverdance dancers hold their shoulders still should have made me think about my golf swing. And Lord knows that wild Irish beat should have made me think about "tempo." But during the entire performance all I could think about was Graham. Sitting up there, stealing glances at me while I stole glances at him.

It shouldn't have been a surprise when he walked up behind me at intermission, but it was. I sensed the warmth of his body, felt his breath on my hair before I heard him, and every cell, every molecule responded, turned toward him as if by magnetic pull. This was some crazy old-fashioned love!

"You look *so* good," his voice murmured in my ear. Seconds later he introduced us to his sister with almost regal formality. She beamed at me. So she knew.

"He's quite handsome," Lauri admitted once we had returned to our seats. "But I still don't get this not-in-public thing. It's insulting."

"Well," I replied, "we're playing golf together next week."

"Where?" Lauri asked.

"On the coast," I confessed, slightly embarrassed. We almost always played on coastal golf courses or upriver at Tokatee. Sometimes we'd even drive all the way to eastern Oregon, with its bonanza of elegant high-desert courses.

"Uh-huh. Where he won't run into anyone he knows. He should be taking you to his damn country club," she said. "What *is* his problem, anyway?"

"He's afraid his wife will take away his children."

"She can't, Jess. That's why we have *laws*. He's a wimp."

Graham called from his cell phone the moment we walked in the door that night. His sister had given me high marks.

Furthermore, he had a new golf assignment for me. "You're going to need a local golf instructor," he said. "It's always a bad idea for one's . . . friend to do it."

I gasped. He'd almost said "boyfriend" or, knowing Graham, "Significant Other." I was bedazzled.

"So," he continued, "I think you should consider Al Mundle over at Riveridge. He taught at the country club for years. He's the best."

I had heard as much from just about everyone. Whenever I mentioned to experienced Northwest golfers that I was learning to play golf, they suggested I study with Al Mundle. It didn't matter if I was in Seattle, Portland, or Eugene, or on a jet somewhere in between, the response was always the same: Go See Al. For the record, everyone also assured me that Al Mundle was "the nicest guy you'll ever meet."

I made an appointment with him the next day.

As it turned out, Lauri saw Al before I did. When I put her on her plane back to California the following afternoon, tearful as usual, I called out after her: "Next time we'll play golf!" The tall, lean, well-dressed man boarding the plane in front of her turned around and said back: "*Now* you've got your priorities straight!"

That was Al.

When I met Al at Riveridge for my maiden golf lesson, he shook my hand. He had a grip like a . . . golfer. Then he grinned like the bespectacled boy who is forever hiding in the complicated illustrations of children's books, beseeching unsuspecting doting aunties (who would prefer to be *reading Where's Waldo?* to their nieces and nephews) to *find* Waldo.

Al Mundle looked just as mischievous as Waldo, but a *lot* cuter, with his upturned turquoise, genuinely merry eyes, his sweetly sticking-out ears, and a manner that can only be called pathologically humble. As with Peter Croker and Cindy Jones, I liked Al very much right away.

He seemed to like me, too, though I imagine he pretty much likes everyone. Even more mysterious was that he seemed to *know* me.

"Oh, your friend told me all about you," Al said with a sly grin.

"Graham?"

"No, Lauri."

Unbeknownst to me, their plane had had mechanical problems and everyone had to de-board, then wait in the airport lobby for hours. Somehow, Lauri and Al had become great buddies in the process.

Between Al's natural good-heartedness and his surprising new alliance with my long-term dear friend, I felt completely at ease with him. Besides, I had my own Nancy Lopez Golf Clubs. I was ready to hit golf balls! My confidence didn't even fade when Al uttered every golf rookie's most dreaded words: "Let me see your swing."

Without apology or excuse, I drew my three-iron from my handsome new golf bag, stepped up to the pitcher's mound, as it were, forced my errant left palm onto the top of my club, splayed my feet a little, lowered my right shoulder a bit, performed Peter Croker's Excalibur Routine, adjusted my stance accordingly, read the ball Al had placed on the rubber tee for me, expected nothing, then hummed "The Tennessee Waltz" while I hammered straight down for all I was worth . . . and missed the little ball completely.

Golfheimer's again!

I couldn't believe it. This had to be the stupidest game in the known universe! I could *not* believe it. But before my ego could launch a stealth bomber from my limbic brain, Al gently reached over and made the simplest adjustment to my hands: He moved my right index finger a tee's width to the left.

"That'll help stabilize your grip," he assured me. "Try it again."

I did. And this time the ball did what it should have done the first time—it flew a country mile.

Al smiled. And set another ball on the tee. I took another swing and hit it almost as well as I had the first. Al set down another ball. I hit it, too. A familiar smugness came over me. I was, I know, careening dangerously close to the faux golf confidence that had overtaken me in Montana. Fortunately, Al took care of that.

"See that lipstick on your collar?"

For one strange moment I thought he was going to accuse me of something. I turned and looked. There on my left shoulder was a russet-colored comet of Lancôme *Interdit*, which in French means "forbidden."

"I'm doing something I'm not supposed to, aren't I," I asked Al. He smiled and nodded.

"You're not rotating your upper torso properly. You know how the tub of a washing machine turns? Well, I want you to cross your arms on your chest with a hand on each shoulder and just turn like that tub does."

He demonstrated for me. Then I tried it. With my arms held close that way, the turn felt compact and sure.

"Okay," Al said after quite a few turns, "that's good. Now I want you to lean over from your waist and do some more turns."

"Do I turn my head, too?"

"No. Just your upper body. A complete turn."

I tried it.

"Okay, now you're pulling up again when you turn to the right. That's why your right shoulder keeps colliding with your mouth."

Al had me stand up straight again and repractice the basic turn. Once I had it right, I tried it on a tilt.

"Now you've got it," said Al.

"This is a lot like when Peter had me pretend to turn in a barrel," I told him.

"Peter?"

"Croker. An Australian golf pro who teaches back East. Have you heard of him?"

"No, I haven't," Al replied, "but I can see that he knows what he's doing. Your grip is great, and so is your stance. We've got a lot to work with. You just need to practice turning. We'll take you through the basic steps: the turn, learning to swing your arms back and through, hinging and unhinging your wrists, short swings when you take it halfway back— that's for your chip shots, your full swing, and putting. Those are the fundamentals. The way I see it there are three parts to learning golf: the fundamentals, how to play the game, and the mental game. Golf is eighty percent physical in the beginning, then once you're a good player, it's eighty to eighty-five percent mental. Good golf is a lot of practice all the time. That's what I tell my kids."

His kids?

"The kids on the University of Oregon golf team—I'm their trainer. I was flying to one of their tournaments the night I met your friend."

So not only did I have the best golf teacher in the Northwest, I had my own alma mater's golf instructor, too? *And* the best women's golf clubs on earth!

What next?

12

fish & chips

"I think it's time for you to see the birthplace of golf," Graham announced without warning.

"You mean . . . *Scotland*?" I said, stunned. I was already suffering from mild shock because we were about to spend our first weekend together—at least our first planned weekend outing. We were in Graham's car driving west to "the coast," as we call Oregon's long white ribbon of beach. What the evening held I could only guess. At the moment I was trying not to think about it.

"Scotland," Graham confirmed with a nod. "And all its great old courses."

"But . . . but . . ." I literally sputtered, "I'm not *good* enough yet!" I also didn't want to go by myself, but having been raised by a southern mother I wasn't about to ask Graham if he intended to go with me.

"Oh, the goal wouldn't be to play," he assured me. "It would be a historic adventure, back in time with your kith and kin, lassie," he added in a surprisingly authentic brogue.

I smiled. Graham rarely broke character.

"The Maxwells were Lowlanders," I demurred. "Golf, as I understand it, is a Highlander's game . . . laddie."

"Aye, but 'tis a Scot's dominion, 'tis, 'tis. Moreover, it's a Scottish *woman's* game."

According to Graham, women had been playing golf in my ancestral homeland since the late 1700s.

"But Scottish women really took to the game about a hundred years ago," he explained. "And rather than fight men to be members in their golf clubs, the women started their own. They built their own clubhouses, too. Elegant Victorian things. Many of them still exist, at St Andrews, Troon, Aberdeen, Carnoustie, Gullane. Almost all of the great courses have great women's golf clubs, but nobody knows it. I think you should go on a reconnaissance mission and see for yourself."

"When?" I asked. I was pixilated.

"Early September," Graham replied firmly. Clearly, he had a plan. Then something occurred to me.

"Umm . . . ," I began, "when will your divorce be final?"

"End of August," he answered without missing a beat.

"So," I ventured, incorrigible curiosity, and raw terror, chasing my words, "would ye be going to Scotland then, too, laddie?"

"No," Graham said. "It's a woman's journey. I think it'll be much more powerful for you to see this by yourself."

I could barely contain my disappointment. Damn. This man was so confusing. Was he interested in me or wasn't he? Was he the throwback gentleman I thought he was, waiting until he was legally single . . . or not? One minute he was whispering meltdown messages in my ear, the next he was sending me halfway around the world by myself. I was almost angry.

"So," I said sweetly, forcing my mind away from danger, "tell me about the course we're going to play today [*you infuriating excuse of a boyfriend,* I added to myself]."

"Sandpines?" Graham answered. "Well, it's a links course . . ."

"Like in Scotland?" I just had to add.

"Like in Scotland," Graham confirmed. "Except it's not a true links course. The terrain makes it look like a links course, but it's really not because the fairways go all the way from the tee to the green. On true links courses they're broken up. You're playing over desert, sand dune, gorse. And on Sandpines there are more trees. Coastal pines everywhere, a lot of sand, and a lot of lakes, which makes it real pretty, especially for a public golf course."

In 1993, in fact, *Golf Digest* magazine voted Sandpines the Best New Public Course in America. Within two minutes I saw why. The course was perfectly beautiful. Its serenity quotient reached Zen levels much more quickly than even Tokatee or Crosswater did. How interesting. I was beginning to discern subtle variations in golf course terrain, whereas, in the beginning, they all had looked pretty much the same.

Part of Sandpines' charm was its generous horizons. The course was as open as the sky above it, except for its here-and-there fringes of pines. What especially drew my eye was its palomino palette, the creaminess of vast rhomboids of sand, the feathery gold of its beach grasses. All of it kept fresh by its vivid fairways and greens, and the blueberry summer sky.

Graham put on his black golf Stetson and we climbed out of his sturdy SUV. The moment we did he began scanning the terrain. For one insulted moment I thought he was scouting for anyone he might know who could catch him in the act of being in public with a woman-who-was-not-his-soon-to-be-former-wife. When a look of relief crossed his face I feared I was right, but Graham proved me wrong.

"Another miracle," he said. "No wind. I almost didn't bring you here because when it's windy, which it often is, this course is a bitc . . . challenge," he corrected. I appreciated his old-fashioned manners, and suspected that his pre- and post-divorce ethics were born of the same gallantry.

"So, what was the *first* miracle?" I asked.

"Getting a second chance with you," he said.

I was speechless. He must have meant running into me again at Tokatee.

"Were you . . . hoping to see me again?" I ventured.

"Yup," he said without looking at me. With a hand on the small of my back, he gently directed me into Sandpines' modest pro shop.

While I excused myself to visit the ladies' room, Graham approached the attending golf pro, to whom I overhead him say, "Two nines." I was grateful that Graham was so familiar with golf's curious lexicon and chose to use it. He was an excellent on-the-ground golf guide.

On the wall above the toilet was a surprise: a poster published by *Golf Digest* with pictures of the country's most environmentally correct golf courses. Sandpines was one of them. This again brought up the aspect of golf that weighed most heavily on my conscience, that, in fact, had kept me away from the game for years: its deleterious effect on the natural world. Just mentioning that I'd taken up the game brought monsoons of "How could you's" from my many conservationist pals.

Then, while having dinner with my parents one evening I made a disparaging remark about this issue and was taken aback by my stepfather's response: "You haven't done your homework." In the last five years, he said, the PGA had made remarkable upgrades in its environmental standards for golf courses.

I brought the subject up again while speaking with one of my own personal eco-heroes, Terry Williams, environmental director for Washington State's Tulalip tribe, former director of the Environmental Protection Agency's Office of the American Indian, and one of the most informed and powerful conservationists in the Northwest. To my complete surprise, Williams said that the Tulalips had just completed construction of a golf course on their reservation lands north of Seattle. "Our standards were high and absolute," he told me, "and they were all met."

It was with renewed spirit that I left the ladies' room for the ecologically enlightened challenges of Sandpines Golf Links.

Graham wanted to warm up on Sandpines' Wee Links Putting Course, a neat little putting practice range.

"Your short game is . . ." he began.

". . . seventy percent of your score!" I sang.

"Very *good,*" Graham said. He was, I think, genuinely impressed. A few strokes later he suddenly looked up. A strange new expression was on his face, something on the order of fear edged with amusement.

"My golf coach has The Yips," he reported, and he said it in a voice doctors use to tell patients they have only a few weeks to live. "He quit smoking and his short game went to hell."

The Yips. That mysterious dreaded golf disease. I'd heard the term a number of times, but no one would tell me what it meant. The first time someone mentioned it I found it so charming I wanted to get The Yips just to be able to say I had them.

"No you don't," every serious golfer told me. But that's all they would say. They wouldn't say why I didn't want to get The Yips and they wouldn't say what in the world The Yips were. The closest I came to a working definition was from my golfer pal Eric Ottem, who probably only spilled the beans because he's a talker. But all Eric said was: "The Yips are when you totally lose confidence in your putting ability." Then he added, ". . . Now don't ever use the Y Word around me again."

"Here's my chance," I thought. As nonchalantly as possible I said back to Graham:

"So, what are The Yips, anyway?"

There was a deathly silence. When Graham finally spoke all he said was: "So how do you like them Ducks?" Meaning our local university football team, meaning The Yips case is closed and if you value your health you will not go there again.

I didn't.

For fun, and I hoped for more private time together, Graham had rented a golf cart. He had also bought iced teas for us while I was in the rest room. Unsweetened. How did he know? We took off beneath a Bauerware-blue sky with a light cloud batter spreading in the west. A storm could be coming, I knew. But at the moment the air was sun-warmed and Mediterranean and so was I.

Graham stopped at the first tee box.

"I'm going to use my three-iron," I announced.

"Driver phobia?"

I nodded.

"Well, you'll use your driver when you're ready. Sure is a pretty one, though," he said, and placed a hand, fingers splayed, around the round bronze club head of my Nancy Lopez #1. My stomach did a quick polka, and so did a few other things. Ah, God. How would I ever get through this game?

Graham hit one of his perfect drives "off the blues," as he put it, referring to the blue tees, which were, in fact, the second-longest tee-off position. I thought of Cherry and Bill Gillespie and pronounced Graham's drive "surgical." He smiled.

I, of course, played off the red tees, which according to the scorecard meant that, in the end, Graham would have played fully a thousand more yards than I had. I felt like a cheater. Nonetheless, I hit my three-iron well and we motored right to it. I made a second decent hit, my ball landing neck-and-neck with Graham's drive.

"Heart golf," he said.

I was touched.

"Heart golf," I repeated. "How romantic."

"*Cart* golf," he repeated, laughing. "As in, we can drive the cart to the same place for both balls."

"Oh."

"It's a nice thought, though," he added, and patted my hand.

Since it was the only club I was truly comfortable with, I used my three-iron again. And smacked my ball right into a bunker. Graham decided to use his five-iron, but cleaned it first by sliding veins of dirt out of its horizontal grooves with the sharp tip of a wooden tee.

"Does it make a difference if an iron's clean or dirty?" I asked.

"Dirt puts a spin on the ball," he replied. "Cleaning it makes it fly through the air with the greatest of ease."

Indeed, soon Graham was on the green. Three hundred and twenty-three yards in two shots. Not bad.

I managed to dribble my ball out of the bunker, only to three-iron it into a second sand trap.

"Bunker Babe," Graham declared. If I could have purred I would have. With some struggle I finally sank my ball. I had scored 8 on a par 4. Graham, however, parred the hole. We were off to a fine start.

His second drive was a 240-yard wonder. Using my three-iron again, I bungled my drive, but launched my second and third shots. My confidence soared. Graham noticed. "In golf we live and die on every shot," he said.

He was not pleased with his drive off the 2nd tee.

"I hit it fat," he almost spat, "which also means I hit it short."

"Fat and short is rarely a winning combination," I agreed.

I bumbled my way to the green and scored a 7. Despite his imperfect drive, Graham parred that one too.

He knighted the 3rd hole, a "par-five long dog," meaning that it doglegged, in this case to the left. He hit a scorching 250-yard drive down the middle.

"I got my game back!" Graham declared. "I turned the club a quarter inch in my grip so the club face was parallel to the swing path. Now it's just booming out there. With only one minor adjustment, I've got my game back!"

Graham's joy was contagious. In two shots I drove my three-iron within 15 yards of his triumphant drive. But then I took three more piffling, dribbling shots to catch up with him. Five shots to make 300 yards on a par 5 with another 112 yards to the green. Oh, bother!

I salvaged myself with some fancy Cindy Jones putting and ended up scoring an embarrassing 9. Curiously, Graham bogeyed the hole. Swallows dipped and swooped and some kind of warbler warbled from the nearby pines.

"Damn Disney golf," Graham said with a rare grin. We were both pretty darn happy.

"I think I'll try my three-iron," I proclaimed on the 4th tee.

"Or you could use your three-iron," Graham suggested.

"Naw, I think I'll stick with my three-iron."

"Oh, come on. Be brave. Use your three-iron."

"Oh, all *right*. The three-iron it is."

My heart felt as big as the great outdoors. I gripped my faithful favorite club, performed my Excalibur Routine, took my stance . . . and blasted the ball down the fairway.

"Great shot!" Graham all but yelled.

"But it went in the bunker again!" I wailed. Graham was surprised.

"Well, it was still a good shot. Or a 'goo shaw,' as a Japanese business colleague of mine likes to say."

Graham drove another Graham Slam. More than 240 yards.

"Poetry," I said. I knew Cherry would have said as much.

I hooked my drive badly.

"It's my tempo," I told Graham. "I can't get the . . . swing of the swing."

"Pitch it onto the fairway and live to hit again," Graham advised.

I did just that. Then, still using my three-iron, I remembered Peter's edict to "hit down," and did so and sent my ball flying.

"Goo shaw!"

But something was wrong. My rhythm. My sense of it. I *had* no sense of it. If I thought about it I could get technical and hammer down, but something was way off with my basic beat.

"I need a swing song." I sighed.

"A swing *song*?" Graham answered. "You mean like Ally McBeal's theme song?"

"Sort of. It's more like a song with a strong rhythm you can keep in your head while you swing."

"How about 'Yankee Doodle'?"

"*Too* strong," I said, laughing. "Too fast, too."

"*Night on Bald Mountain*?"

"Too scary!" I cringed at the thought.

" 'The Little White Duck'?"

"Hmmm. The rhythm's right." I took a few practice swings to it. "Naw," I said finally. "Too embarrassing. What if I become a famous girl golfer and the press wanted to know my secret. I'd have to lie."

Sadly, I was forced to continue playing without a swing song. Even sadder, I continued to chop and slice.

"Veg-O-Matic," Graham concluded.

It took me five shots total to get on the green, then four more to "hole it," as he calls making a putt.

Graham shook his head. "You went extreme on that one."

A lovely lake on our right cheered me up. Until I realized that it was a seriously long water hazard on the next and 5th hole, from the blues a 178-yard par 3. Seeing my distress, Graham went first. His drive splashed exuberantly into the water. Grimacing, he tried again. And drove it to the edge of the green, a classic chip shot setup.

"Better," he muttered, then he drove us to the lake and produced a long, ingenious tool with a metal circle at one end. It reminded me of a giant Easter egg dipper. Graham fished around in the lake with it and finally produced his lost golf ball.

"Fish and chips," he proclaimed.

At that point my own budding game fell apart. Probably because at that point I managed to hit myself on the back of my head with my nine-iron. Hard. Finally, I clawed my way to the green, and after a bout of truly lamentable putting I whined: "I don't want to keep score anymore."

"You don't have to," Graham replied. "I'll do it for you."

Those are the moments. Those are the details. Those are the little courtesies, infinitesimal in the wider scheme of life, that sink the putt of love deeply and forever into the God-shaped hole. If men only knew. I, for one, will never forget Graham's perfect offer of care, though I doubt he himself was aware he'd made it.

He was quite aware of his next drive, which was, by any measure, awesome.

"Right where I aimed it," he allowed. "I think I'm getting my game back." Suddenly he waxed poetic. "A dogleg right, pines on the left, and a second shot to a well-protected green. The scent of the ocean, foghorns, and U.S. Coast Guard sirens on the tee. And thee," he added to my delight. "It just doesn't get any better."

Amazing what a good golf shot will do for a man. He steered our cart along the cart path with reckless abandon.

"What kind of bark stuff is this path made of?" I asked.

"Bark," Graham replied, which sent me into a gale of giggles. Then I had a sobering thought.

"I wonder if that would have seemed so funny if I hadn't just hit myself on the head with a golf club."

In the end, Graham bogeyed the 6th hole with a 5 and I managed to scoot in with a 6. I was ecstatic.

"Do you know what the most feared three words in golf are?" he asked me.

"Umm . . . snake, bear, and Yips?"

"No, 'You're still away.' "

Graham regarded our scorecard.

"The seventh hole is five hundred sixty-six yards from the blue tees," he said. "Uphill. Which effectively turns it into a six-hundred-yard hole at least." He was not pleased.

I looked at the long, straight fairway edged in pretty knuckle swales. Suddenly I was very happy to be there, in that fresh coastal air, my trusty three-iron in my hands, playing *golf*. It was a defining moment. The first moment I felt as though I was actually playing the game, not practicing it. Of course, I aced my drive, which flew far, straight, and true, my best of the day.

"Well *struck*," Graham said. Then he more than matched it. "I'm just so damn happy to have my game back," he added.

We merrily drove toward our merry drives. My second shot was a good one, too, mostly because I was still hitting my irons and still remembering to hammer down.

"Look!" I cried. "I made my first divot!" My shot had left a long triangular gouge in the black, grass-topped soil. It looked like a piece of chocolate torte edged in crushed pistachio. Which reminded me of food. Which reminded me of drink. Which reminded me that I'd drunk my entire big cup of iced tea and needed the ladies' room again. My eye caught a plastic urinal-shaped container resting in a metal bracket on the frame of the golf cart.

"I wish they had those for girls," I said absently.

Graham followed my gaze. He suddenly looked alarmed. "What??" he asked, blinking.

"That urinal-thing. I wish they made them for girls."

"*That?*" he asked, pointing.

"Yes."

"I can't believe that you . . . you can't possibly think . . . this is a *gentlemen's* game. *That*, my dear, is a divot repair tool."

"It *is?*"

"Yes. It's filled with a sand-and-grass-seed mix. You sprinkle it on your divot . . ."

". . . so it doesn't turn into a sand trap?"

Graham rolled his eyes.

Sandpines' 8th hole was not his idea of a good time.

"Now, this hole, bless its soul, is an asshole," he announced with uncharacteristic coarseness.

"You mean the guy who designed it was mean?" I asked.

"No, *it* is an asshole. If you hit it long you're in La-La Land, if you hit it short you're in the bunker. It's only a couple of hundred yards, so you have to be careful."

To complicate matters, a Pacific zephyr had just come up. Graham settled on a seven-iron. As fate would have it, he hit it just right and his ball landed mid-green with Pro-Am profundity.

"Huh," he said. "I just hit a seven-iron a hundred ninety yards. I usually hit it a hundred twenty yards. I hit a three-iron a hundred ninety yards. That means it's a two-club wind. The way to play wind is like this: If you're hitting into the wind, hit low; if you're hitting with the wind, hit high. A two-club wind is a pretty big wind."

"*A two-club windddd,*" I crooned, "*is a pretttty big wind . . .*"

Graham joined in.

"*And a two-club windddd . . . is bound to waaannder!!*"

He went on to putt for birdie—a "birdie in the wind," he called it.

"That sounds like Silly Putting to me."

My own tee shot was short, then I hit it onto the hillside,

then I hit it onto the hillside again, then I hit it onto the green. Two putts later I was in. The numbers weren't great, but they were falling.

Our last hole was a long par 4, almost four hundred yards from my red tees. Graham addressed his ball. When he did, the pines emitted a strange chattering sound.

"Squirrel?" I said.

"Ladybug," Graham countered.

"*Ladybug??*"

"Well, there was a ladybug on my ball. I had to move it."

He was surrounded by some kind of beachy bunchgrass that looked like hair transplants.

"Bad ones," Graham added.

A brindled wild bunny emerged from it and stared at Graham for a few beats too long. Things felt quirky. Off. Sure enough, Graham hooked his drive badly. He hadn't done that all day.

"Tryin' to hit it to the moon," he admonished himself.

When I addressed my ball everything suddenly seemed to go quiet. I knew that feeling. I'd experienced it fishing many times. Either your mind falls into some sort of cosmic vortex, or some kind of cosmic vortex subsumes your mind. Maybe it's what Shivas Irons called "True Gravity." Whatever it is, when it happens you know you are hovering on the precipice of an otherworldly event. All you can do is buckle your seat belt and hang on.

From the center of that eerie stillness, I swung my club. And hit my ball. Well. Graham knew it right away.

"That was a good shot," he said while my ball was still airborne.

"I knew I'd hit it well," I said. "Because everything went still."

"And you just know," he said back.

"Yeah," I replied. "You do."

"Then I have a little gift for you," he said, this man of endless surprises and nearly no clues. With that, he presented me with a package of golf balls. My first.

"Read them," he instructed.

"*Read* them?"

Graham nodded. I did. They were a brand I didn't recognize, a brand I'd never played before, and a brand that amounted to a wonderfully literary vote of confidence: Maxfli.

I've never bought another brand since.

I enjoyed golfing the Oregon coast so much that I took my eleven-year-old namesake naturalist nephew, Jesse, there a few weeks later. He likes golf, but the previous summer I'd gotten him hooked on fly fishing. Naturally, his first response to my invitation was: "Do we get to fish, too?" Naturally, I said yes. I confess to also bribing him with a special lunch at the Heathman Hotel in Portland, whose French chef happens to love fly fishing, too.

"They fly fish in France?" Jesse asked.

"*Bien sûr!*" I replied. "That means 'of course.' Here's another good one: What do you think 'tweet' means?"

"Uh . . . bird?"

"Nope. Trout."

"'Tweet' means 'trout'!" Jesse said with a laugh.

"Yep. And it's spelled t-r-u-i-t-e, but you don't pronounce the 'r'. The French like to put a lot of extra letters in their words in case they need them later to make new insults with."

"How do you spell 'golf' in French?" he asked.

"G-o-l-f, as far as I know. We can ask the hotel chef."

"I don' know eenytheeng about galf," Chef Philippe Boulot insisted. "But I love fly feeshing!"

His Normandy accent bounced around the already festive Heathman Restaurant. "*Alors,*" Philippe added with a shrug, "zere is no feesh left in France. Zat's why I'm in Portland. Deed you know," he asked Jesse, leaning over our table until they were practically nose-to-nose, "zat zis hotel ees on *Salmon* Street!?

"So," Chef Boulot said, suddenly straightening up, "how do you like your feesh?"

"On my fishing line!" Jesse answered happily.

"Ha! Good answer. Well, me, I like my feesh a certain way. For instance, I want it with the skin on. Even in Portland it's hard to find."

That declaration tempted me to order the *Provençal Fish Soup au Pistou*, with its piscatorial panoply of Oregon mussels, clams, salmon, rockfish, and prawns. But who could resist the *Grilled Chinook Salmon in an Oregon Truffle Demi-Glacé*.

"*Oregon* Truffles?" Jesse asked.

"They're gathered wild in zee forests," Boulot assured him. "And zey match *eeny*thing in Provence!"

The sauce's deep woodsy musk perfectly countered the salmon's rich, persimmony meat. I almost wished Jesse and I hadn't already shared one of *Andrew's Crab Cakes*, dense with sweet Oregon Dungeness crabmeat and served with tropical fruit relish and red curry and ginger sauce. Or the *Marinated Halibut Salad* with organic cress, a coconut-lime vinaigrette, and salmon caviar—Jesse called it "bait." But neither of us was too sorry to order an awesome *Bittersweet Chocolate Crème Brûlée* made with South American El Rey Bucare chocolate, as demanded by the Heathman pastry chef and Philippe's sweeter half, Susan Boulot.

Visions of coastal golf courses helped me haul my formerly lean self back into our car. Within half an hour we passed the turnoff to Pumpkin Ridge Golf Club.

"That's where Tiger Woods accepted Nike's forty-million-dollar offer to go pro," I told Jesse. His eyes widened.

"Cool."

Cut out of the Willamette Valley, the green hills of Pumpkin Ridge's Ghost Creek Golf Course carry the buckling charm of any good Celtic countryside. The valley is laid down between the Coast Range and the Cascades, and you quickly see its original allure to weary farmers arriving on the Oregon Trail.

And to golfers.

The eighteen-hole, par-71, 6,989-yard championship course earned *Golf Digest*'s vote as its number one new public course in 1992, the year before Sandpines did. It quickly attracted national attention by hosting the 1993 and 1994 Nike Tour Championships, then went on to hold the 1996 U.S. Amateur and the 1997 U.S. Women's Open. In 2000, Pumpkin Ridge will host the U.S. Boys' and Girls' Junior Championships, marking the first time the two events will be held at the same facility.

Wisely, course designer Bob Cupp let the land's natural features rule. The first few holes were built out of farmland, the rest out of woods. Many native Oregon maples and firs were left standing, and wetlands reign throughout. The left side of the 4th hole, a long par 5, hugs a protected marsh— knock your ball in there and it's gone.

"You know, Ghost Creek Golf Course is very ecological," I told my nephew. "It's fully certified by the Audubon Society. Well," I added, "it's not the real Audubon Society, it's a group in New York, I think, that started a really tough environmental rating system for golf courses. I don't think the real Audubon Society is very happy that they've used their name."

With a child's perfect logic, my nature-loving nephew cut directly to the heart of the matter by saying: "But it's still a really good thing, right?"

"Sea-run cutthroat are the most beautiful—and least known— trout on the coast," Milt Fischer told us as we hiked along the North Fork of the Nehalem River. It's a short coastal stream, the North Fork, seventeen miles that wander through conifer forests and small dairy communities that produce Oregon's famed Tillamook cheeses. As promised, Jesse and I were making an afternoon fishing stop before continuing on to our main destination, the new links course at Salishan Lodge in a little coastal hamlet called Gleneden Beach, about an hour's drive south down Oregon's liturgical north-central coast.

Fischer had driven us a few miles upstream from River House, his modest fly fishing lodge where world-class anglers like news anchor Tom Brokaw and writer Tom McGuane book annual pilgrimages. Mostly they come for Fischer's legendary winter steelhead trips. The walls at River House are filled with photographs of gleaming arm-long wild steelhead, which are, in fact, oceangoing rainbow trout. We were there for wild cutthroats, much smaller trout but hearty fighters nonetheless. As usual, Jesse caught the first one—as usual, in our first five minutes on the water.

As usual, I just kept casting. Fischer's special polar shrimp fly made miniature hot pink meteors in the air above me. It looked like a little angel flying around up there. That made me think of church music, and that made me think of the CD I'd been listening to lately, Van Morrison's wonderful *Hymns to the Silence*. Before I knew it I was singing the words to my favorite song on the album, "Be Thou My Vision," a slow old spiritual whose rhythm happened to follow the natural four-count cadence of my casting:

> *Be Thou my vision, oh Lord of my heart*
> *Nought be all else to me, save that Thou art*
> *Thou my best thought in the day and the night*
> *Waking or sleeping, Thy presence my light.*

Three counts on the backcast, three counts on the fore, three counts on the second backcast, three counts to release. It was perfect. It was also, I suddenly realized, a waltz.

"It's a *waltz*!" I hollered.

"What is, casting?" Milt asked, bemused. "Yeah, I guess it is."

"Casting is *and* the song is! And that's the secret to Sam Snead's golf swing!"

"Sam Snead fly fishes?"

"*NO!* He hums 'The Tennessee Waltz' to himself every time he swings. And I'm going to hum 'Be Thou My Vision' every time *I* swing from now on!"

"So, do you still use hooks?"

We were sitting in the office of Grant Rogers, golf pro at the Salishan Lodge. Jars of sauerkraut-in-the-making stood inexplicably on his window ledge, a photograph of St Andrews hung on the far wall. Naturally, I thought Rogers was referring to my golf swing.

"Oh," I stammered, "I'm not really good enough to use hooks."

"Well, I'm getting good enough *not* to use them," Rogers replied flatly. "So far I've had three trout voluntarily hold my fly in their mouths—just the fly; I'd snapped off the hooks. I reeled one in all the way to the bank."

The Oregon Golf/Fly Fishing Connection again. We were there to hear Rogers talk about Salishan's new Scottish links course, but his unexpected treatise on hookless fly fishing had thrown a red herring into our plans. What had driven him to such extremes, anyway? Jesse was beyond intrigued.

"Well," Grant whispered, leaning forward over his desk almost at a putting angle, "I was fishing this little stream somewhere in Wyoming, I forget, and I got this big brown on. He was giving me a good fight when, out of nowhere, this other huge brown trout took a torpedo run at my line and started biting it! With her teeth!! I figured she was his mate, and I felt so bad I released my fish immediately . . . and vowed never to use a hook again."

Rogers arched his eyebrows and ran a large hand through his bunker-colored hair. He looked a little crazy. Then he spread his long fingers out on his desktop as if to center himself and grinned and said to Jesse, "Want to see my new golf course?"

A few years ago Rogers had redesigned Salishan's eighteen-hole course to give it a more traditional Scottish feel, which made perfect sense, etched as it is into the dunes there on the wind-bashed edge of the state. Rogers had agreed to give us a private tour. Pretty soon he had parked our golf cart beside the 11th hole.

"Now this is a long par three with a small target," Rogers began. "The ocean is right over those trees, so if you hit a wild slice, it's gone."

He was, I noticed, scanning the very blue sky for something. I thought he was bird-watching.

"No wind," he announced. "Wind is a big factor on the coast, just like in Scotland. Pilots call the pro shop to find out about the wind here. One woman actually crashed her small plane in that sand trap over there. I was the first one there. She crawled out with a martini glass in her hand—had been drinking since Portland."

His eyes narrowed and he looked quickly over both shoulders.

"I don't have much time this morning," he said. "They're after me, again. They're always after me. Let's go play the last four."

I confess I was expecting a more traditional tour guide. But then, out of 27,000 U.S. golf pros there are only 171 PGA Master Professionals, roughly equivalent to a Ph.D. in golf, maybe two. Rogers is the only Master golf pro in Oregon. The man knows his stuff. But he also had a meeting, and so opted to show off the last holes on the back nine, the most linkslike of all.

Our cart flew past wind-bent evergreens and great mops

of beach grass gleaming in the sun. It was a beautiful day. We made a turn to the south and suddenly there *was* wind, thrillingly cool and scented with sea minerals.

"Look at that view!" Rogers commanded. It was hard not to. Our golf cart had just completed its third orbit around the 16th tee. The view *was* stunning. To the north, white surf lines broke up miles of royal-blue shallows. Long, flat, and endless, the Oregon coast at its best. I was glad the ocean was behind the tee—who could concentrate?

"That's Cascade Head farther north there," Rogers said. "The Indians used to send their braves there for vision quests." If they could have time-traveled they would have witnessed a miracle: From the back tee Rogers sent his ball rocketing over two car lengths of sandy links-style rough, splitting the fairway 270 yards out. On a 332-yard par 4!

"I had a tailwind," he demurred.

So did I, but I barely cleared the rough. Jesse, the newest golfer among us, flubbed his first hit, then sailed his second over the imposing thicket that so badly truncated the fairway. So this was the kind of true Scottish links course Graham had described to me.

"We built that rough," Rogers said. "We built up the sand dunes, then planted the dune grass. Really, the whole place is just sand dunes, sand, sea grass. Doesn't it look like it's been here forever? Now," he added, "you can see how tucked in that pin is, right?"

The tiny green was surrounded by sea grass and dunes, with bunkers on the left and right sides of the hole. Rogers made the green on his second hit. It took me two more shots and Jesse three. The green was fast and tricky to read. Nonetheless, Rogers putted for birdie and made it. I double-bogeyed and so did Jesse.

"All right," Rogers said, "onward to the terrifying pro tees of the seventeenth hole."

We had to hike up to them; they were set tight and steep into a terraced corner of the woods. I'd never seen anything like it on a golf course. The target was all but invisible, a 291-yard par 4 from the back tees.

"It's short, but difficult," Rogers counseled, "because there's extremely high grass on both sides and bunkers on each side."

The one on the right was a sod-faced bunker with a vertical face of four or five feet.

"This is a ten-ball golf course," Rogers confided. "People usually lose ten balls here. One of our best junior players scored a twenty-seven on this hole." Still, Rogers parred it.

The finishing hole was a long dogleg left, a 370-yard par 4. "The interesting thing about this hole is how many ways you can play it," Rogers said. "Long hitters could try to hit the green. Or, you could be conservative, or try to play it in between. Distance isn't the object here; it's more strategy and direction. But you have to hit your first one in play."

That's when I started humming. "Be Thou My Vision," indeed.

Rogers made the green in two. Hitting from the front tees, I still took forever to get close to the green, even with my new swing song.

"What is that?" Rogers asked. " 'Amazing Grace'?"

"Close," I said. Then I told him. "So, what's your swing secret?"

"Oh, that's easy," Rogers replied. "My mother used to write me notes so I could stay home from school and watch the Three Stooges with her. I learned everything I know from them."

"Okay," Jesse said suddenly. "I've got it!"

"Got what?" we wanted to know.

"My swing song." At that he grabbed his five-iron like a microphone, wiggled his little hips like a hooked-trout-meets-Madonna, and sang:

Like a surgeon! Cutting for the very first time!
Like a surgeon! Kidney transplants on my mind!

Then he slammed his club into his waiting ball and sent it on a fast track to green-land.

"Weird Al," Rogers said approvingly. "Right up there with the Stooges. It should work."

My swing song didn't that time. I ended up in the worst bunker I'd ever seen. Ever. It was more of a crater, really—another links-style sod-faced bunker built into the hill that supported the green; its vertical face was taller than I am.

Seeing my concern, Rogers stepped in front of my ball, turned his back to the green, and, holding the club head of his sand wedge almost parallel to the ground, swung hard. The ball barreled past his left shoulder and landed two feet from the hole.

"When in doubt," Rogers concluded, "hit the ball backwards."

After his meeting, Rogers treated Jesse and me to a putting lesson on Salishan's practice putting green, which he designed himself. You have to pass under Highway 101 to get there, and while you play, cars blast by above with unnerving regularity.

"One time I was giving a student a lesson down here," Rogers told us, "and without saying anything I suddenly picked her up and threw her over there," he said, motioning to a flat area by a tree.

"Why?" Jesse and I wanted to know.

"Well, in my peripheral vision I saw the shape of a car coming toward us through the air. I barely got my student out of its path before it landed on the putting green. When it did this woman got out and said, 'God told me to turn the wheel.'

So I said back to her, 'And God is telling me to take away your car keys.'"

Rogers's putting lesson was easy. And impossible.

"Look at the target, not the ball," he told Jesse, "and keep looking at it."

"You sound like my high school geometry teacher," I told Rogers. "He told us that the way to draw a straight line on a blackboard is to keep your eye on where you want the line to end *while* you move the chalk. Every time he did it his line was perfectly straight."

"There you go," Rogers agreed. "He was a master."

"Since we're putting," I ventured, "can you please explain to us what The Yips are?"

Rogers grinned. But the light in his eyes glinted steel.

"I'll tell you everything you need to know about The Yips," he replied. "Here it is." He folded his tall frame over until he was eyeball-to-eyeball with both Jesse and me, and he said . . .

13

....

the yips

"Don't get 'em."

14

the girls of summer

"I might have been an athlete."

So begins *Full Court Press*, Lauren Kessler's trailblazing book on the University of Oregon's championship women's basketball team. When I read that perfect first line I winced. I might have been an athlete, too, if childhood sports had been available to my generation. A sprinter, maybe, like my father. Maybe a quarterback. When our neighbor and high school star quarterback, Pat Moore, taught me to throw a bullet I could do it immediately. And I loved how it felt.

I would, at least, have been a surfer, raised as I was at the beach in Southern California. I did become an ardent Boogie Boarder, awaiting the jumbo waves of a tidal condition called the South Swell with surferlike anticipation. I felt the same thrill surfers did, too, racing down the two-story glass faces of near-tsunamis that would just as soon eat you for breakfast as give you a free ride. But surfers got to ride waves standing up; a girl, if she dared to ride at all, was obliged to do so lying on her belly like a reptile.

Girls didn't surf.

Like Kessler, at my high school girls didn't have a wrestling team, or a track team, either, and we didn't play baseball, basketball, football, soccer, hockey, lacrosse, or golf. The joys of team sports, or of just playing an active, organized game together out-of-doors, did not belong to the girls I grew up with. So when it came to finding girlfriends to play golf with, I was at a loss.

My sister, Heather, was a budding golfer, mostly because the law firm she works for treats its attorneys to an annual golf retreat at Pebble Beach—enough to inspire anyone to pick up the club. Alas, Heather lives in Northern California. Rande lives in Seattle. When I tried to talk her into coming down for an Oregon golf weekend, she cited her single perfect drive at the Old Works course in Montana and, in a voice that sounded pretty much like Death Valley, said: "I've already played golf."

She did, however, volunteer to drive the golf cart if ever I wanted to play a round when she was visiting.

Soon after, I happened to mention the scarcity of golf girlfriends to my banker, Jenny Thompson, vice president and manager of Bank of America's main branch in town. Her face broke into a radiant grin. "I play!" she said triumphantly. We made a golf date at Riveridge for the next afternoon.

I called to make a tee time, then I asked to be transferred to Al Mundle's extension. "I'm playing my first all-girl golf game tomorrow!" I yelled in his ear. "With a real tee time and everything!"

Al was waiting for Jenny and me in the pro shop when we arrived. I must say, he seemed a bit like a proud father. He shook our hands and wished us well, then said to me: "Remember, turn your torso, follow through, photo-finish."

I nodded solemnly, and we were off.

"Do you want to rent a golf cart?" I asked Jenny as an afterthought. She smiled, as usual, but her eyebrows said, "You've got to be kidding."

"Katharine Hepburn always walked," Jenny reminded me.

"*Cool* clubs!" she said as I heaved my Nancy Lopez bag into a pull cart.

"I don't play well enough to deserve them," I confessed, "but I started playing better once I got them."

"Where did you get them?" she asked.

I told her. And was amazed to know that she knew exactly who Graham was. "He's a heavy hitter," she said sotto voce.

At the first tee, Jenny examined my clubs more closely. "Can I try your driver?" she asked in the tone little girls use for asking each other if they can borrow a prized Barbie outfit. She took a few practice swings.

"Wow, it feels *so* good!" Jenny cried. "What a perfect grip."

I explained all the field testing with *real* women that had gone into Nancy Lopez clubs, and how Nancy herself personally helped with every design and even named every product herself. Jenny listened with rapt attention, then said: "I'm getting some."

A week later she did.

By all accounts, that sort of executive decision-making is characteristic of the kind of woman taking up golf these days. Golf, of course, has long been a man's sport, but it's also been a businessman's sport.

"I *have* to play golf," Jenny told me. "For work. You wouldn't believe what kind of deals are cut on the golf course."

I was most curious about Jenny's golf swing, and tried to observe her carefully. But there wasn't much time. Jenny walked up to the ball and clobbered it. Just like that. Bang. Gone. I shouldn't have been surprised. At the bank she's quite capable of transferring funds for you, looking up an account balance, finding a forgotten ATM card PIN number, and answering a phone call in the same nanosecond.

With a Nancy Lopez driver in her hand, Jenny was dangerous.

And intimidating. It's one thing to play golf with a girlfriend; it's quite another to play golf with a girlfriend who can really play. By the time I addressed my ball I was almost shaking.

I was also using my good old three-iron.

"Why aren't you using your driver?" Jenny inquired.

"Well, I really don't know how to use it yet."

"Oh, come on. You've *got* to start using your driver. You can't play golf without it. Here," she said, and thrust my #1 driver into my hands. "Try it."

With extreme mortification I rebagged my three-iron and took a few sissy swings with my driver.

"*Swing* it!" Jenny commanded with smiling impatience.

I was afraid she'd step in and swing for me if I didn't. But all I knew about drivers was that they still felt like too-long, out-of-control UFOs in my hands. By some miracle I remembered that Al had said something about a driver swing being a "sweep," as opposed to the hammering swing an iron required. So I took my stance again, did my Excalibur Routine, took a big breath, swept my driver through the air . . . and missed the ball altogether. I felt my face go crimson.

"You're too close to the ball," Jenny instructed. "Remember, a driver's longer. Here." She backed me up a little. It made a big difference. The driver now fell comfortably at the point where my hands naturally hung.

Jenny reset my tee a little higher. "Easier to hit," she explained.

"Why do you have a tee stuck in your shoelaces?" I asked.

"That's where I keep 'em so I never lose 'em."

I refocused, then took another swing. This time the ball did a turbocharged leap and stayed up there for what seemed like whole minutes.

"Whoa," I said. It really was impressive.

"Told ya," Jenny said back with her winning grin.

Her powerful swing outgunned me for the rest of the game. But she wasn't perfect, either. Sometimes Jenny's drive would slice badly, which, I admit, made me feel a little better. She was also *really* fun to play golf with and took her game a lot less seriously than Graham did—probably than any male golfer does, for that matter.

Riveridge is a beautiful place. Its creators, Ric and Debbie Jeffries, built their golf course out of classic old Oregon farmland. Their family home, a handsome brown-shingle farmhouse, anchors the property—you can see it from the parking lot. Horses feed in adjoining pastures near some holes. Fruit orchards line others, abloom in spring, heavy with pears and apples in summer. A red barn sits charmingly in a field by the 9th hole. Jenny regarded it with a sly smile, hooked a thumb in a belt loop, and announced: "Why, ah could hit the broad side of a barn from here!" Instead, she hit the green. When she was on she was awesome. Jenny Thompson was definitely one of Peggy Kirk Bell's "little girls who can hit it a mile."

We had so much fun playing our first round of golf together that Jenny asked me to play with her on a bank-sponsored team in an upcoming fund-raiser "scramble." She said that we'd play with two other teammates—both (gulp) guys.

"We'll partner up and each partner will hit," she explained, "then you see which ball went the farthest, and the partner who was short will play it. That's a scramble."

Sounded scrambled to me. It also sounded scary.

"I'll play if we can be partners," I said. Jenny grinned and said, "Of course."

The scramble was held at a suburban country club, where I was to meet Jenny. When I arrived, hordes of serious-looking golfers shouldering golf bags were marching resolutely to the outdoor registration tables. I was not ready for this.

Jenny was sipping an iced tea when I found her. "Good thing they're giving us golf carts," she said, wiping her brow. "It's too hot." She was right. It was one of those cloudless, blue-sky August days that turn the sun into a brute. To our chagrin, our golf cart had no roof.

"We're gonna be scrambled eggs by the time this scramble is over," I said.

"Or fried," Jenny added.

We had been teamed up with a couple of veteran golfers who happened to be cousins. They were pleasant enough, but even in the heat we could detect a little Good Old Boys Club ice. Jenny and I were glad we were a team; a good time was guaranteed regardless of how poorly we played.

Both guys outdrove us by a country mile. That meant that they were always far ahead of us. And *that* meant that Jenny and I were basically in a different movie. Theirs was high drama, ours was low comedy. But we couldn't have guessed how funny it was going to get.

In a scramble, you have to pick up the shorter driven ball as you progress toward the far one. Jenny and I swiftly turned that task into a kind of golf cart polo. I drove, gingerly at first, while Jenny leaned over and scooped up the unplayable ball on the run, as it were. After our first successful attempts we gained confidence. And speed. With each success I accelerated a little more, in a gleeful attempt to see how fast we could go and still pick up the ball.

I'd like to blame what happened on the heat.

We had stocked our cart with as many liters of ice-cold designer water as we could find, but no amount of liquid could keep that merciless sun at bay. You'd sweat out anything you drank as soon as you drank it; that's how hot it was. Hot enough to make us immediately motor into the shadow of the nearest tree each time it was the guys' turn to hit. Hot enough, when we were reduced to pausing beneath a mere sapling, for Jenny-the-Banker to sigh and say: "Even the branch manager couldn't get any shade out of this thing." Hot enough that by the end of the day we'd emptied every one of our bottles of water, and several iced teas from the roving beverage cart, and neither of us had had to visit the ladies' room once.

Surely, it was hot enough to impair the judgment of a

ruthless, roofless golf cart driver who, for all intents and purposes, had been hovering near heatstroke for hours.

What happened was this: We were on the way to pick up a ball—mine, of course—giggling and gaining velocity as we went. Jenny had assumed Ball Pick-up Position and thus was leaning halfway out of the cart, arm extended, eye on the ball. Except that the dead-eyed cart driver, now an expert at deciphering the actual form of an actual golf ball from the usual fairway flotsam and jetsam, realized that the "ball" Jenny was about to scoop up was, in fact, a leaf. A leaf with its silvery underside exposed—hence the round, white golf ball–like shape, which was especially deceptive when viewed at a distance from a moving vehicle. At about the same split second, the cart driver noticed in her peripheral vision the image of the *real* golf ball, which lay in the grass at, oh, a good 45-degree angle from the ersatz golf ball leaf. The driver's reflexes kicked in and she deftly altered the course of the cart . . . but failed to warn her polo partner before doing so. The driver's final image of that now historic girl golf event is of her friend Jenny, still grinning broadly, a small leaf clutched in her right hand, being propelled out of the cart in midair and looking very much like what she would look like if she were, say, going around and around in a clothes dryer just for the fun of it.

The other unforgettable moment in that desiccated golf game was just as heroic, if less dangerous (miraculously, it should be said, Jenny wasn't harmed by her golf polo roll). And the moment, I must say, was mine. We were playing the 16th hole, out of patience, out of sunblock, out of water, and in every way very nearly out of gas.

The hole was a monster, much like the one at Sandpines that had elicited scatological mutterings from the normally courtly Graham. It was a short par 3, but from all tees you had to carry about 110 yards over a cavernous, water-filled ditch bisecting the fairway, which, at the same time, doglegged severely left to a steeply raised green. It was far too easy to overshoot the green, but if you shot short you'd get ditched.

The first of our scrambling macho cousins teed off; his ball splashed down just about in the middle of the water. Our second guy-team member drove his drive right into the ditch, too. Jenny-the-Fearless took the mound and *almost* made it across, but her ball caught the inner lip of the ditch's outer edge, then rolled painfully downhill into the drink.

It was all up to me.

I had noticed that the drives of all three of my teammates had one thing in common: They had been struck with nine-irons. My only comfortable club was still my three-iron, and this was the most uncomfortable tee-off I'd faced so far. My teammates assured me that a three-iron would hit too long for this drive; I'd end up in Wyoming.

I regarded my Nancy Lopez golf bag, then shut my eyes. "Nancy," I murmured, "please, be thou my vision. Which iron should I use?"

Use your nine-iron! The words were so clear, the Queen of Women's Golf might as well have been standing right there beside me. Never mind that I'd had no luck whatsoever using my nine-iron. Never mind that my teammates probably already thought I had gone bonkers because they'd caught me mumbling something into my golf bag with my eyes closed. Never mind all that. Saint Nancy had said it, I had heard it, and that settled it. A nine-iron it would be.

With trembling hands I drew the prescribed club from deep within its metal nest. The light clanking it produced sounded like a prayer wheel. I took my tee from my shoelaces, where Jenny had taught me to stow it. I pressed my ball into the tee's small hollow, held it there with my thumb the way Graham had taught me to do, then pushed the tee's sharp wooden tip into the grass for a faultless tee-up. I spit on my hands for no known reason, and looked at them. I could visualize Peter Croker's blue markings as if he'd just drawn them. My hands also appeared to be glowing.

I took my grip. Forcing my left palm hard over the top of my club, I said to myself: "It's an iron. Hammer, don't sweep." Then I executed an uncommonly smooth Excalibur Routine and addressed the ball. I lowered my right shoulder. I splayed my feet. I tucked under my derriere. I thought "Elephant! Elephant!" and I saw the Tokatee Coyote's half-dead shrew falling pendulum-like in the air above me. I coughed. I took a few of Al Mundle's washing machine practice turns, planned a complete follow-through, and—since I was Mundle's ward, and "ward" is what his name means in German—I asked *Gott in Himmel* for the reward of a well-deserved photo finish. Then the golf secret that Babe Zaharias had shared with Peggy Kirk Bell rang in my head: "Use Your Big Muscles."

If the whole tournament hadn't ridden on this one stupid shot, my teammates would have abandoned me long before now. As it was they just stood there, Jenny as patient as a nun, the guys as expectant as fathers-to-be, while I awaited the arrival of Shivas Irons's Fertile Void. Nobody said a word.

I took a breath, blew it out my mouth as I had witnessed Peter Croker do. I read and reread my ball, which, thanks to Graham, was inscribed with the cheering phrase "Maxfli." I memorized the two feet in front of me. I tried hard to expect nothing. Then I heard Ethel Hunter's chicken-scratch southern drawl holler, "Keep your damn head down!" Cherry Gillespie's strong tenor sang out "Surgical!" and the sweet voice of my own dear nephew, Jesse, warbled out "Like a surgeon! Cutting for the very first time!" Somewhere in the trees behind me, crows cackled with delight. Finally, Van Morrison's *dementia illuminati* began to scroll behind my eyes.

I took my cue. My nine-iron whistled like a hawk as it passed my ear, its crafted Lopez head found its mark, and my ball exploded in the general direction of the ditch. Then it lifted, like a raptor on a thermal. Effortlessly levitating. Hanging like a holograph in my line of sight, the little white dot kept going. Over the ditch and through the woods it flew, gaining momentum with every millisecond until, at last, it found its own True Gravity and began to fall slowly back to earth. When it landed, it landed pure, pin-high in the fringe on the flat of the plateau that was, on that hell-bent hellhole, the green.

My teammates, of course, were ecstatic. High fives were had by all. So this was what it was like to win the big game by sinking a last-second 3-pointer or batting someone in in the bottom of the ninth. It felt great. But I felt feverish. Between the heat of the day, the warmth of divination, and the fire of potential eternal damnation for having almost killed Jenny *and* blown the shot, I needed to lie down. At the very least I needed a cold, stiff Evian. Fortunately, the tournament was almost over. As if by preternatural decree, Jenny stepped up and putted us in for birdie, long putts being her forte.

"I think," she said, "it's because I played so much miniature golf as a kid. But you know what . . . I still miss the windmill."

A few days later another girlfriend called: She was ready to play golf. Candace Sellers Cappelli. A consummate female CEO, she'd run companies for years and was currently a principal and partner in her own corporation. Like Jenny's, Candace's mind cuts to the chase so fast the horse gets whiplash. Like Jenny, she always has a smile in her voice and she's pretty much game for anything . . . "as long as I get to wear a cute new outfit." As brainy and successful as she is, style is key to Candace.

So it shouldn't have surprised me that she already had a new golf ensemble, put together, of course, around a very short skirt. *And* she had a brand-new set of golf clubs—Nancy Lopez, of course, on my recommendation.

"Umm . . . have you ever played golf before?" I asked her.

"No. But I want to *look* like I know what I'm doing out there."

Candace is based in Portland, Oregon, but she and her husband, Bruce Cappelli (whom she calls "my fabulous husband Bruce" so often that I myself have come to refer to him as Bruce-the-Fabulous) also have a, yes, fabulous second home on the McKenzie River. Thus, I scheduled our maiden golf voyage for a Saturday afternoon at Tokatee.

Though Candace was raised in a golfing family and certainly meets the business requirements for becoming a woman business golfer, as I've said, she wasn't one. However, in true executive fashion, once she got her golf clubs she spent hours hitting golf balls in her backyard prior to our golf date. So we decided to begin our golf-girlfriends career with a practice session at Tokatee's driving range and on the putting green.

"But lunch and wine first!" Candace insisted.

It has always amazed me how important great food is to Candace, given that she's as lean as a teenager. She wears a size 6—we both do—but on Candace a 6 somehow looks like a 2. Needless to say, her "cute new outfit" truly was.

"I *refuse* to wear those mannish golf clothes!" she exclaimed as I arrived in her driveway. Imagine her surprise when she saw that we were wearing essentially the same golf ensemble that day: short black pleated skirts, white T-shirts, and black cardigans. I wore black tights and sneakers, Candace wore little white anklets and sneakers. Now, *that's* a girl golf outfit.

Adjacent to the Tokatee pro shop is a nice many-windowed snack bar, which Candace and I had to ourselves. We ordered tuna sandwiches. To quell her golf nerves Candace also ordered a glass of chardonnay, which arrived at our table in a strange little carton.

"Wine out of a *box*?" she proclaimed! "I'd call this chardonNAY! Next time we bring our own."

Nonetheless, the wine did the trick, preparing my proud but uninitiated golf pal to face the general golf course public. We bought our ball tokens, and the golf pro recognized me. "You're back," he said, though I couldn't quite read his tone.

"You're . . . Rick, right?"

"Right," he said. "Been practicing?"

I could almost hear him thinking, "I hope."

"Oh, yes!" I replied. "In fact I've been *studying*. At Riveridge with Al Mundle."

"Al's great," Rick allowed.

I nodded. "Played a whole game the other day," I added, then realized how it sounded and flinched.

Rick grinned.

"A *whole* game. That's great. That's just great. Well, here are your John Daly tokens."

I couldn't believe he'd remembered.

"Hey, okay!" I sang back. Then I had a powerful thought. "Well," I added, "have a nice day . . . and don't get The Yips!" and happily watched the smirk melt off Rick's handsome face like the Wicked Witch of the West.

(I resisted the urge to add: Heh-heh-heh-heh-heh!)

"What did he mean by that John Daly comment?" Candace wanted to know once we were outdoors.

I recounted my first Tokatee token experience, explaining that I'd asked Rick if they hired John Daly to stomp on all the golf ball machine tokens.

"Sort of like grapes?!" Candace chirped merrily. "I've always wanted to do that, married to an Italian and all."

For a moment I wondered if her midday cocktail had made her a little too relaxed, then I assured her that using special coins for rituals like Visiting the Golf Ball Machine was very important to golfers, who are, I was now convinced, a superstitious lot.

"Well, I was thinking that this whole token thing is weird," she replied. "I mean, why can't they just hand you a bucket of golf balls, for Pete's sake?"

"At least for John's sake," I added solemnly.

Candace was quiet for a moment. Then she frowned. "What are The Yips, anyway? They sound fun."

"Heck if I know!" I told her. "No one will tell me. I think they sound fun, too, and for the longest time I wanted to get them . . . until *the* coolest golf pro at Salishan forbade me to even think about getting them on purpose. Whatever they are, they're really bad."

"Oh, for heaven's sake. How bad can anything called 'The Yips' be? I mean, maybe if they were called 'The Cramps' . . ."

". . . or 'The PMSs'!"

". . . or 'The Cellulites'!!"

"Eeee-ooo . . . now *those* would be horrible! We do *not* want those!"

"No, we do *not* want The Cellulites," Candace agreed. "But I think it would do some good for *men* to get them every once in a while so they'd understand how hard it is to get rid of them!!"

I agreed. "All I can say is that The Yips had better be at *least* as hard to get rid of as cellulite or these guys are total wusses!"

"Exactly," Candace concluded as we dropped our John Daly golf tokens into the golf ball machine, gathered our respective buckets (two each) of balls, and headed for the driving range.

It was another stellar summer day. The distant fizz of summer insects energized the morning, an American kestrel hunting low nearby gave it a wild business-as-usual feel. There were, thank goodness, no crows in sight.

Still, Candace's girl golf career had an alarming debut: She missed three balls in a row. Completely. Whiffed every last one of them. Even with a five-iron, her backyard practice club of choice.

I managed to hit mine, but not well.

"Well, at least we have the best *legs* on the course," she said gamely, then teed up again, and missed yet another ball.

"Ow!" she wailed. "Do we get points for breaking a nail?"

I teed up and sent another ball slightly heavenward, but I made an ugly gouge in the grass in front of my tee doing it.

"You notice," I offered to diffuse some of my friend's emotions, "the pros never take a divot *before* they hit the ball like I did."

"Well, what do they know!" Candace replied. There is nothing on earth like the myopic support of a good girlfriend.

Candace teed up again and hit the ball this time . . . about two feet. Suddenly Rick-the-Golf-Pro's voice issued forth from the loudspeaker: "Mr. Smith and Mr. Tyler on the tee."

"Oh," Candace said, relieved. "I thought he was going to tell us to get off the green and stop embarrassing ourselves!"

"Well, at least we're out here *trying*," I said. "Even Michelangelo said if people knew how hard he worked to master his art they wouldn't think it was so wonderful."

Candace looked at me as if I was the one who'd had too much wine, then she teed up again. Again, she hit a sad little dribbler. By now her face was flushed with mortification. She glanced around nervously to see if anyone else on the course had been watching her. Mercifully, no one had. Every guy in our 180-degree visual field—and they were all guys—had his head down in deadly concentration.

"Don't worry," I offered as soothingly as I could, "the only golf swing any golfer cares about is his own." Which is what Graham had told me early on and which I now knew was true.

Candace took a big breath and closed her eyes. You could almost hear her mind telling itself to Get It Together. Moments later I was treated to an awe-inspiring sight: the in vitro process of another sensitive and strong woman willing herself away from the edge of a cliff.

Candace's eyes flashed emotions. In five seconds flat I witnessed the broken vessel of defeat heal and right itself, then by pure, self-induced alchemy be transformed into the metal that got my friend where she is today. She exhaled.

"All right," she declared with stand-back vigor, "I'm ready to go long."

To my astonishment, Candace marched her dainty feet over to her Nancy Lopez bag (which, appropriately, she had ordered in black) and drew forth her driver. I winced. Was she ready for this? Without a word she teed up.

Blawp-ping!

She nailed that ball.

Va-plonk!

She nailed that one, too.

Swish-a-bam!

Her third drive catapulted down the driving range with such force we both looked at her club head to see if it was still there. It was. And it continued to slam golf balls into the thin summer air for half an hour.

I was so impressed I almost forgot to hit the rest of my own practice balls. When I did I launched the first two, sliced the second, turned the third into a rocketing worm-burner, as grounders in golf are delightfully called, then caught fire much as Candace had. We continued to hit golf balls long and well nonstop, and both earned, that first practice session, far more hits than misses. Swinging almost in tandem, we smashed our last balls into oblivion, then looked at each other with panting grins, a difficult feat that tends to make anyone who tries it look like an Irish setter after a round of Frisbee. I looked back at the pro shop and was pleased to see that Rick was watching us. He had to be smiling.

"Well [pant-pant], shall we retire [pant] to the putting green?" my triumphant friend inquired.

"In[pant]deed," I said back.

"Oh [pant], good," Candace replied. "I have a [pant] virgin putter!"

She hadn't inaugurated her putter yet? This *was* a big day. I was afraid to tell her how tricky putting is, despite its miniature golf appearance.

"Putting is the one thing I was good at as a kid," Candace informed me. "And chip shots. Pitch and putt, that's my game."

Momentarily forgetting that her dad was a golfer, I was surprised that she even knew the term "chip shot." And was even more surprised to see that she was quite good at it.

"But you know," Candace said after making several elegant shots, "there's kind of a fine line between a hinged and an unhinged wrist."

"Not as fine a one as between a hinged and an unhinged mind," I thought. What is it, anyway, that makes golfers become so emotional over a poor drive? Why *do* we live and die on every shot? as Graham so aptly put it. And what was it, really, that allowed my dear friend to redirect her mind-set from the precipice of the Valley of the Wimps into the warrior state of One-Who-Refuses-to-Give-Up? Even the pros are known to pitch both fits and clubs when things don't go their way in a tournament. Golfers, in general, can go utterly ballistic on the golf course. The worst example I've heard of was the story a friend told me about a man who was playing with his golf buddy of twenty years and wound up hitting a drive that came to rest at the foot of a tree. The golfer became so enraged at the position of his ball that he threw his club at the tree. The club "wrapped around the tree and snapped in two and one of its broken ends rammed into his golf buddy's chest and killed him. It was in the *New York Times*," my friend told me.

What *was* powerful enough to overcome both fear and anger? I knew love did it automatically, even adolescent puppy love. Pulling what I call a Charlie Parker can do it, too—playing the inside of the game by sliding into a transcendent state of mind "detached from outcome," as golf mystics like Shivas Irons and Peter Croker put it.

Candace had added one more force: pure will. She was *not* going to let a stick and a ball get the better of her, and that was that. Suffice it to say, she appeared almost serene on the putting green after her heroic performance on the driving range. Once she'd made her sixth or seventh putt she turned to me, smiling, and said something that spoke directly to golf's inherent balance, which the game could probably teach us all if only we gave it half a chance. "I think the short game calms you down," said Candace, "so you're not in fairway murder mode anymore."

Finally my golfing attorney sister, Heather Meeker, found a weekend to fly up from Northern California and play golf with me. Only four days after my practice session with Candace. I was beginning to feel like a regular golfer with real golf buddies. I booked the last tee time of the day at Tokatee. Rick, the golf pro, had assured me that if we played any earlier we'd be sandwiched into an already tight lineup and therefore have to labor under relentless pressure from the golfers behind us to play what Graham referred to as "ready golf" (i.e., no long preswing rituals or endless practice swings). I was probably as grateful for the tip as the golf pro was for my having taken it.

Heather and I both flubbed our first tee shots. Both of our second drives were better, as were our third. All I remember about the entire 4th hole was the Western bluebird that landed on the sunlit branch of a fairway fir and glowed there like a russet and cobalt miracle. I so love bluebirds.

Heather and I both hit power drives off the 5th tee. Both of us were already tiring in the hot sun, too. "It's one of the mysteries of golf," my sister intoned. "I work out, I eat right, and I can barely finish eighteen holes. So how do all those big fat guys drinking beer do it?"

As my baby sister teed up on the 6th hole she made the sort of startling, offhand comment only an intellectual property attorney can make during a golf game: "Did you know that golf ball dimples are patented?" I considered answering that Fred Couples's dimples should be, too, but was too taken aback.

"Why?" I asked instead.

"Because the patterns are especially designed for specific aerodynamic effects. Also, none of them are symmetrical."

I don't know why this fact bothered me so much, but I felt a little like what the conservative German physicist, Max Planck, must have felt in 1900 when he discovered that atoms don't radiate energy in a neat, consistent stream but in weird little exuberant bursts which he named "quanta," Latin for "packets." To maintain an orderly vision of the world we need to believe that fundamental things such as atoms and golf ball dimples are predictable. It was, I am sure, the shock of Heather's new information that completely messed up my next drive.

And my putting. The 6th green was elevated and the hole was set at its apex. My asymmetrically dimpled ball had deemed to land at the bottom of the incline, and so, for that matter, had Heather's.

"Well," she said, "as someone recently told me, 'If you hit it too hard you have a chance of getting it in the hole, but if you underhit you have no chance at all.' "

"Did you learn that at Pebble Beach?" I asked.

"Yeah," she replied, "but you should really call it 'Spanish Bay'—that's its real name."

Oh no. Another golf inconsistency.

"I'm a rookie!" I wailed. "I need golf ball dimples to all be the same and I need Pebble Beach to be Pebble Beach! They're all I've got!"

It surprised neither of us that I overputted the 6th hole, then landed in a bunker on the 7th fairway. Heather's shots just kept getting better and better.

On the 8th I took a moment to evoke Peter Croker and re-instigated my Excalibur (Preswing) Routine. And got my game back.

"Nice drive!" said my sister. Then she thought a moment. "Could I try your driver?"

She had rented a set of . . . well, rental clubs and hadn't been happy with them.

"We're spoiled. When you rent at Pebble Beach they give you thousand-dollar Callaways and a Big Bertha."

"Well," I said smugly, "see what you think of those Nancy Lopez specials."

Heather loved them. Luckily for her, her birthday was only a week away.

In the end, it was neither my budding golf skills nor my ultracool golf clubs that drew the most applause from my sister; it was the fact that I had been the one who had made sure that we didn't miss our tee time. So impressed was Heather that a week later there arrived in the mail the following affidavit, which, while somewhat humiliating, bears noting if only to applaud the deeper disciplines of golf. To wit:

My name is Heather Meeker. I am a corporate lawyer. I declare the following to be true.

On August 27, 1998, I played nine holes of golf with my sister, Jessica Maxwell. Jessica arranged for a tee time of 4:30 P.M. We arrived at the course early enough to hit a small bucket of balls on the range before starting our round of golf.

That's it. That's my declaration. Well, I must say, you don't seem impressed. But to anyone who knows Jessica, my statement would be unbelievable, outrageous, fantastic.

Jessica has always been, shall we say, one of the "promptness-challenged." Once she moved to an island near Seattle. Again, you seem unimpressed. But this island is accessible only by ferry, a ferry that stops running promptly at midnight. When Jessica told me this I figured she would buy herself a dinghy or rent an apartment in Seattle. But never did I ever consider the possibility that she would learn to be on time. In this respect, I am glad to say she did not disappoint me.

So when Jessica told me she was learning how to play golf I had only one thought: "WHAT IN THE NAME OF SWEET HOLY MOTHER OF GOD ABOUT THE STARTERS!?" The starters would never stand for it. To play golf, one must arrange a tee time. To play golf, one must arrive before the tee time. Golf starters, as all golfers know, are not born, but hatched in some infernal timeliness hell decorated with giant Daliesque dripping, ticking clocks and fiery sundials, where starters-in-training decapitate the dilatory with giant, searing seven-irons and smack their lips at steaming platters of the tardy, whom they dress and stuff, mouths agape, with range balls. I figured my sister would remain forever on the driving range because she would never actually play a round of golf.

So you can imagine my surprise when she called to arrange the golf outing, and said, "Well, it will take twenty minutes to get to the golf course, and we're going to have lunch first, that will take an hour, plus an hour to get to the restaurant and back, and we need thirty more minutes to pick up Mother . . . I'm working backwards, here . . . and I want to hit some balls on the driving range first to warm up . . . so we'll have to leave at noon." I have to confess I was nearly speechless. Even more amazing, we showed up early for our 4:30 tee time. When the starter said go, we went.

> *I am going to have to stop making those snide re-*
> *marks about PGA charities. I used to snicker at the*
> *idea of old white men helping the needy by teaching*
> *them a country club game. But anything that can make*
> *Jessica get somewhere on time is bigger than all of us.*
>
> *I declare the above to be true, to the best of my*
> *knowledge. No, really.*
>
> Heather Meeker, Esq.
> Attorney at Law

As if I hadn't had enough of lawyers, two weeks later another one arrived: David Belasco, a patent attorney and a friend of Valerie's, my psychologist sister and Jesse's mother. Both she and David live in our California beach hometown. David, a good Jewish boy from New York, had never been to Oregon.

One of the great liabilities of living in the Northwest is that people want to visit you in the summer. Family members, friends, and friends of friends and family like David. You get used to it. I swiftly learned to turn all guests into golf partners, willing or non.

David was game for anything. We drove to the coast, ate at all the best restaurants, and I taught him to fly fish. Though he was a self-proclaimed nongolfer, I also said I'd teach him to play golf—at least golf swing fundamentals as I understood them. Off to the Riveridge driving range we went.

At my insistence, David teed up first, borrowing my driver. His natural stance reminded me of a giraffe. His arms were as stiff as . . . well, giraffe legs. I didn't know where to begin. I suggested he practice Al's old washing machine turns. He did so cheerfully. I said he might consider splaying his feet a little. He did, and looked even more like a giraffe, albeit a very handsome one. Anxious to hit the ball, he went ahead and pulled back, and then, with alarming force, he slammed it hard. It flew an even 250 yards. On his *first* hit. Secretly, I took a lot of the credit. The rookie finally turns teacher.

David's next half-dozen hits were almost as perfect as his golf swing was lamentable. I was baffled. Could I really be *that* great of a teacher? Had a little of Al Mundle's genius rubbed off on me?

David asked me to hit while he watched.

I teed up, took a few practice swings, went into my backswing . . . and hit a horrible piffling shot. I teed up again. This time I launched the ball, but it hooked badly.

"Why don't you try closing your club face a little," David suggested. As with Candace's chip shot expertise, I was surprised that he knew golf terminology. Dutiful student that I am, I took his advice. My next shot straightened out considerably. Still, it hooked.

"Your left arm is a little loose," David offered. "Try stiffening it."

"Really? I've never heard of that."

I tried it anyway. The ball flew true, as did the half-dozen that followed. My final drive pretty darn much split the fairway, landing at the 200 yard flag. I narrowed my eyes. I suspected my new pal wasn't telling the truth, the whole truth, and nothing but the truth.

"Okay, where did you learn all this?"

"Just watching golf on TV," David replied with a shrug.

"Come *on* . . . What's the real story?"

"Well," he said slowly, "my grandmother used to own a country club on Long Island," he confessed, "and when I was young I used to caddie there."

"You were a *caddie*!? No *wonder*!" I hollered. "You're a really good teacher!"

He smiled a cat-with-the-canary smile.

"And," he said, "I guess that makes you the Star of David."

15

a lesson with
nancy lopez

The call came in on the cusp of spring.

I had spent fall and winter on The Plateau, working on my golf swing with Al Mundle anytime he could see me. My car knew the way to Riveridge so well I once ended up there when I was supposed to be going to the airport. Truly, I had been a good golfee, listening to Al closely, doing whatever he thought needed doing. We had worked on upper-body rotation. We had worked on swinging back and swinging through, on hinging and unhinging my wrists, on a "photo finish." We had done short swings, then moved into full swings. I had discovered that I'm a kinesthetic learner who needs to feel what something is supposed to feel like before my body can faithfully replicate it. I had practiced my short game. Oh, had I practiced my short game.

And I hadn't improved a bit. Such is the nature of The Plateau. I was, in the truest sense, expecting nothing. Al commiserated. "The first year," he confirmed, "is atrocious."

So when the call came in it was as if God were talking and the person on the other end of the line was just moving her lips: Nancy Lopez would see me. My patron golf saint, Nancy Lopez, would meet me at the LPGA Ping Tournament in

Phoenix the following week. Nancy Lopez would sit and talk with me about golf. And, if there was time, Nancy Lopez would even give me a golf lesson. It was a good thing I was already sitting down.

When I checked into my hotel, the young receptionist noticed my golf clubs.

"Nancy Lopez just checked in with *all* this golf stuff that had her name all over it," the girl said. "Is she that important?"

"She's *the* First Lady of Golf," I replied.

"Well, I hate golf . . . so I wouldn't know. But she was *so* nice."

Nancy was scheduled for a meet-the-fans event at a local golf store. It had been arranged for me to observe so I could see how she interacts with the public. I half-hid behind a table of golf balls and did just that. What I saw right away was something so remarkable it took me half an hour to understand what I was seeing. Nancy was seated at a table, pen at hand, ready to sign all manner of golf products. The evening was designed to promote her line of golf equipment. Fans bought visors, mostly. Mostly they just wanted a chance to shake the hand of their golf heroine. They approached Nancy with their eyes beaming shy adoration. And, wonder of wonders, Nancy would beam it right back at them. Finally I realized she methodically put herself in the place of gratitude, not superstardom. If I could read auras I know I'd see that Nancy Lopez is surrounded by crystalline light. That, in fact, she broadcasts it like a healer.

"What's your name?" she asked a baby riding her father's hip. "Mine aren't babies anymore," she added wistfully. "My baby is seven."

Her voice, too, is healing. Soft, warm, and unhurried, like the morning moving into afternoon. Her eyes smile as much as her mouth does, and she looks deeply into the eyes of everyone who comes to see her. All the while, her hands make nothing but kindly, inclusive gestures. Beautiful hands. Really, the hands of an artist.

"Hi!" say a mother and a teenage daughter.

"Hi!" Nancy returns. "You both golfers?"

"I'm not," the mother says.

"Why aren't you?" Nancy asks.

"I'm her caddie," the mother laughs. Then they talk about golfing in the dry Arizona heat.

"I feel like I swallowed a gallon of dust," Nancy confides as if she's talking to her girlfriends. "I'm gonna practice early tomorrow, before it gets too hot."

Four fellows from England are next in line. They are besotted with Nancy-Love. They ask her to pose with them for photographs. Nancy immediately moves to the other side of the table and stands with them, utterly elegant in a long white ribbed silk sweater and black crepe palazzo pants. At the moment, she does not look like a golfer.

"This is good practice," she says. "At five-thirty in the morning I have a *Vanity Fair* shoot with Se Ri Pak. Of course, I've already been on the cover—my friends glued my face on Demi Moore's body when I was pregnant," she says, laughing.

This shared intimacy impresses the Englishmen to no end. Like the mother and daughter, they begin to talk golf with Nancy.

"My dad always said, 'Don't panic till you get there. You might have a shot.'"

"I had a caddie who always said that," Nancy answers. "In England."

A woman runs up, breathless. She's just gotten off work.

"Oh, I just *love* your swing!" she effused. "I just *love* that you finished two under. I always end up in the sand traps!"

"Well, I just named a sand wedge after my dad," Nancy offers. "Everything in my line is named after important things in my life."

"That gives it *real* meaning!" the woman replied.

"Yes, it does!" Nancy answered. "Golf's a family game. I love it. I've always loved it."

The thing I remember from the long drive to the golf course the next day is oranges. I kept seeing them in the streets lined up against curbs.

"Planets," I kept thinking.

As if they meant the stars were aligned. It seemed right that the Ping Tournament was held at the Moon Valley Country Club.

I was an hour early for my meeting with Nancy. I wandered into LPGA headquarters and was thrown off by the room's intensity. The thing was *organized*. This was serious golf.

Soon after I arrived Se Ri Pak, the Korean wunderkind, gave a press conference. I sat in. Someone asked if it helped her to have her sister touring with her.

"Sister is more like best friend," Se Ri said. "She takes care of me a lot. Her thinking and my thinking are sometimes same. She takes care of my clothes, makes easier for me. Helps me a lot."

Se Ri was, I noted, beautifully dressed.

Moments later someone else asked her to "talk about what Nancy Lopez has taught you."

"I meet Nancy Lopez, then I start winning," Se Ri said. "She gives me hugs, talk to me. She knows. She had hard time like me long time ago. I was only Korean player in country who play well. Interview every day, every hour. Nancy knows I was tired, not easy. She tell me if I am not happy with myself, I cannot focus on my game. She told me about herself long time ago, that have to make myself happy first.

Think about things in a good way. Interviews help me, good for me, so happy to do it. I follow Nancy."

Nancy was waiting for me in the country club dining room. We ordered breakfast. And tea. The Arizona dust was still bothering her. Or maybe it was allergies. Or both. Being interviewed was probably not her activity of choice at the moment, yet when I asked her what it was about golf that had so captivated her at such a young age she answered with enthusiasm.

"I think it was when I walked around with my mom and dad."

"Your mother played, too?"

"Um-hm. She played right when I started. And then once I started we couldn't afford for all three of us to play, so it was just my father and me. Mom gave me her golf clubs, then she just walked with me for the exercise.

"But I think that when I first started I thought how special it was to be outdoors. To enjoy the sunshine—and growing up in New Mexico, mornings are beautiful. And there wasn't much smog back then—the skies were so clear. And putting on a pair of my dad's golf shoes—I didn't own a pair yet—just to walk around in them. They were ten times too big . . ."

"So instead of trying on your mom's high heels, you put on your dad's golf shoes!"

Nancy laughed.

"Uh-huh. And I would just walk around on cement. And back then we had metal spikes. And you could walk around and hear that *cliclck-clicklch-chliclck* sound they made. And I loved it. And I was like, 'Dad, when can I get my first pair of golf shoes?' Because the sound of the golf shoes just intrigued me. There was something about it. I just loved it."

"Did it feel like power to you?"

"I don't know . . . it was a sound I'd never heard. And once I got my own shoes, sometimes I'd just walk on the cement to hear their sounds. Which was terrible for your spikes, but I loved to hear 'em. So that was the first thing I liked about golf, just wearing the shoes.

"And then I remember pulling my golf cart, and they had little beads in the tires and you could hear 'em—*shooo-chohcooshhhsoochoo*—there was this sound. I loved it. I heard that sound, I was walkin' on the golf course, and then I could hear my clubs go *clink-clank-clink-clank* . . . and the sounds of that. All that, I remember. I don't notice it much now. I don't know if it was the love I started to have for golf from the very beginning—I just noticed everything about it."

"Maybe that was . . . the music of golf to you? So many sounds."

"Um-hmm. And I think . . . just thinkin' about playing golf with my dad . . ."

She had to stop for a moment. Tears were suddenly running down her cheeks.

"I don't know why it makes me cry . . ."

"Does it always?"

"I never really talked about it. I think it's just special times that we kind of take for granted. The little things. Of just being with your parents. And celebrating the quiet times with them that you don't really have anymore once you grow up. Everybody goes their own way. It was really . . . a great time of my life. That was so special. And I'll never forget it. 'Cause my dad always made it special. You know, he was sensitive. And he always made golf fun. He made it something that I was going to love. I never hated golf at all. It was a great experience for me, just growing up, playing with my dad. Having my mom there. I think that now you don't have those special times. Everybody's always in a hurry. Thinking about them really hits me hard because I think about how I didn't have to worry about anything, I had my mom and dad taking care of me, and I just played golf. And how much I enjoyed that. My dad loved golf. He loved competing. And he loved watching me play . . . all the time."

"He was *completely* with you."

"Uh-huh."

"Was he completely with you especially on the golf course, because it was something you both loved?" I asked.

"Um-hmm, um-hmm," Nancy answered. "Yeah."

"Maybe it was something about the Southwestern landscape, too. There's such an openness here. A peace. There are so many trees in the South and the Northwest."

"I love trees, but when we're in a place where there are a lot of trees my dad always says, 'I can't see very far. I like to see *far-r-r* away.' He's always loved the desert. Even south Georgia where I live—it's beautiful—you're always surrounded by trees. You'll be driving down a road, and you won't remember where you're going. 'Cause every road looks alike. Too many trees for my dad." Nancy laughed.

Did she, I wanted to know, remember what it was like to watch her first golf ball fly away?

"Well, my dad remembers," she said, laughing again. "You know, his first lesson to me was, 'Hit the ball. Don't ever miss it. Every time you take a swing, hit it somewhere.' Which is a good tip to give anyone when they're first starting. And that's what he would always tell me. And he would walk on in front of me. And he said . . . one day a ball came flyin' over his head, and he said, 'Who hit that?' And it was me. He said, 'She might be a little golfer.' That's what he always says.

"I remember the first tee when I hit my first golf shot. On that tee. 'Cause it wasn't on the driving range, it was on the tee. My mom was playing that day and my dad was playing. And I said, 'Dad, can I hit one?' And he said, '*Sure!*' And I remember I got up there and thought, 'Just don't miss it. Hit it somewhere.' And I hit it.

"You know, after you've watched your mom and dad play so long you kind of mimic what they do, and their swing, and that's really what I did. And he was a good player when I started playing. He had a good mental game. And golf is really very mental. You have to know the technique. Everybody has the technique. But whoever wins are the ones who have the mental part right."

Boy, was she right. I told her about how, during my long season on The Plateau, I'd had days where I could hit everything—not very well and not very far, but I could hit the ball.

"Then the next day I couldn't do anything. And I didn't know what happened. I mean, this game is really mysterious!"

Nancy laughed out loud. And kept laughing.

"I mean, once you learn to cast a fly rod, you can not go fishing for six months, then go out there, and you can still cast a fly rod. But with *golf*! It's like . . . juggling raw egg whites! It's not organized! It makes no sense. It drives you crazy!"

"And that's what makes people love it," Nancy said. "You hardly find anybody who plays golf who won't say they either love it or hate it. There's never a [in a wishy-washy voice] 'I kinda liked it.' There's never that. It's a love/hate game. But the ones who love it have the desire to try to hit that perfect shot. Which they probably never will. They'll hit a really good shot, which excites them, but the shot they're looking for, they want to hit it so badly that it drives them crazy. That's how they get addicted. Getting it in the hole. Making a twenty-foot putt. It's like winning the lottery."

"Yeah! Or a hole-in-one. You've had holes-in-one, right?"

Nancy nodded.

"Well, don't you wonder . . . how could it *do* that??"

"I know," she said, laughing again. "For you to hit a shot and for it to go in the hole waay-y-y far away . . . I mean, it's a little, bitty hole."

"There's *got* to be something else going on."

"It *is* amazing when you stop and think about it. I know,

my husband plays baseball. Standing up to a ninety-five-mile-per-hour pitch, he says, is really tough. But golf seems to him much tougher."

A big statement, coming as it does from Ray Knight, a former major league baseball player.

"But I just loved golf," Nancy continued. "From the time I hit that first shot, I just wanted to hit it. Every time. I just truly believe it's a gift from God to play the type of golf that I have been able to play over the years. It's just a blessing that's God-given. You don't develop it."

You have to wonder, I said, how someone is chosen to be given such a gift.

"You know," she answered, in that level, kind voice of hers, "I think everybody has a gift—they just have to find it."

"And," I added, "some people come in with a gift and it's almost too easy for them and they never develop it. There's a real responsibility with a gift. I mean, you've worked real hard to polish yours."

"And I gave up a lot of my childhood," Nancy pointed out. "I chose to practice and play all the time. Even in high school, everybody was like, 'Why do you play golf all the time?' But I *loved* it. And I *wanted* to play golf. And instead of going someplace on the weekend with friends, I'd play golf with my dad. Because I wanted to be a winner. That's what I always said: 'I want to win, Dad, I want to win.' And he said, 'Well, if you want to win you have to practice.' And so I did. And I gave up being with my friends to play golf."

"Was it lonely?"

"Um, it wasn't really lonely, because that's really what I wanted to do."

"So, did you have golf buddies?"

"Uh-huh—mostly boys, 'cause there weren't a lot of girls who played golf. I played on the boys' golf team in high school because there wasn't a girls' golf team. I tried to get on the team in my sophomore year, but they wouldn't let me play because they didn't allow women to play with the guys. A civil liberties lawyer—a lady—came from Albuquerque, New Mexico, and contacted my parents and said to me, 'Why aren't they letting you play on the boys' golf team?' I told her it was because of body contact. She said, 'There's no body contact in golf. I think you should be able to play on the boys' golf team . . . and we'll take it to court.' That was in 1972."

The following year Nancy Lopez played varsity golf. Her team won the high school state championship that year.

"Were the boys happy you were on the team by then?" I asked her.

"The boys on the *other* teams weren't very happy about it. You know, I think the only time it got lonely for me as a golfer was probably my first year on tour. Because I won so much so early, that I went from being age twenty to being someone who was expected to be more mature, and handle the press. And I know that when I first came on tour and I played as well as I did I pretty much alienated myself from the other players. There was a lot of jealousy.

"So I lost my childhood early. And I missed dating and having fun, being irresponsible.

"Even though I'm forty-two now, and I have three daughters, I like to tell jokes, I like to make people laugh, and I haven't reached in my mind that I'm forty-two. Maybe I'm making up for those times I did miss, but I still think young. I've even gone to a Hanson concert with my kids!"

"Did you survive?"

"Yeah, it was great. We got to meet 'em. They were so cute. I sat through the whole concert with my daughters. *Screamed* with them. Danced with 'em. It was really fun."

We talked more about careers and about helping others once you've had success yourself.

"Well, I don't know if my dad taught me, or it's just my relationship with God, but to be mean to somebody . . . that's really tough for me to do. And to wish bad things on some-body . . . that's just not in me. I can be playing with some-body head-to-head. And I want to beat 'em. But if I don't beat 'em, I can't sit there and resent them."

"Well," I offered, "not everyone is that compassionate."

"People would get a lot more out of their lives if they didn't act like that," she replied. "A lot more satisfaction. A friend said to me the other day, 'How does it feel to meet peo-ple and make their day? I wish I had that power. How does it feel?' Well, first of all, I'm a little tougher on my family," she said with a laugh. "They say, 'Why aren't you as nice to us as you are to your fans?' Well, my fans don't make me mad. They're nice to me! And sometimes you're just tired, and you want some sympathy. You're not going to be a saint all the time."

"Well, yeah, but you're giving all the time—all the press you have to do. It's got to be exhausting. It takes so much . . . well, heart."

And then it occurred to me. Heart. Nancy is such a loving person, she makes an *effort* to be a loving person. Did she think that that helped her game?

"Oh, definitely," she said. "I think what helps me most when I'm out there are my priorities. When I tee off on the first hole, I'm thankful I can swing a golf club. I'm thankful I can walk. I just feel *grateful* when I go out there."

Tears flooded her eyes again.

"To sit and complain about your life . . . is wrong. I am grateful that I've been blessed with talent. And I know that I was *blessed* with it. But to go out there and to play golf and enjoy the sunshine and enjoy life, and health . . . I am very sensitive to that, 'cause I work with handicapped kids, and I try to raise money for them. And I see how grate-ful they are even though they don't have their health. They don't sit there going, 'Golly, I can't walk.' So, to see players, golfers, walking around grumpy and mopey, and just look like they're miserable all the time, is awful. I think it's just wrong.

"And so, when I go out there and play golf, I just feel so grateful to have that opportunity. And then it kinda goes back to my dad, and everything he sacrificed for me. When my parents had no money, they worked so hard so I could go play in golf tournaments. But it's down deep—I don't think about it every time I tee it up. It's just there."

I told her, at that point, how inspiring it had been to watch her interact with her fans the night before, how thrilled they were to be truly *seen* and *heard* by her. Nancy laughed. "There are some professional athletes who think that just because they play a sport they're better than everybody else . . . and they're *not*. And they've got to realize that the fans keep us employed. If all of us were crabby and walked around with long faces all the time, we wouldn't have a job anymore. Sponsors wouldn't want us. That's not what it's all about.

"Fans put me on this pedestal, but I just play golf better than they do, that's all. I probably get my attitude from my dad. He's Mexican-American, and wasn't treated that well years ago. But he was always good. And good to people. You know, we've named our new wedge after my dad," she said. "The Domingo. It means 'Sunday' in Spanish. When Arnold Palmer asked me if I'd ever thought about designing women's golf clubs, I said, 'Golly, you're right. Women have been neglected for so many years.' I mean, they made golf clubs for women, but they weren't really golf clubs . . . to me. They had funny, little bitty shafts. And they were *pink*, with flowers on 'em. And women want to be treated like women when it comes to opening the car door, but don't make us look like sissies. If a woman plays golf, she wants to be a good golfer, and she wants to look serious when she plays. So, women needed that attention, paid solely to them.

"I wanted to concentrate on building a club for women that was easy to hit, that felt really good—I've always been a 'feel' player—and that felt powerful and strong. Mine are really forgiving, too. And women get a choice on their grip for their hand size, too. A lady came up to me last week and said, 'Nancy, I got a set of your golf clubs, and I have taken ten shots off my game.' To help a woman seriously improve her golf game—that's really something."

No kidding.

heart golf

It was time for Nancy to go practice. But later that evening she was going to be cooking a St. Patrick's Day dinner for some of her golf colleagues, and she invited me to come over and talk to her while she cooked.

While she practiced I visited with golf pro Lynn Marriott, golf director for the University of Arizona's illustrious women's golf team. I had been told that she reads people's auras in order to correct their swing, and asked her about it. Lynn laughed.

"No, well, it's more an all-encompassing approach. A lot of people think that if they learn the golf swing, and they learn all the technique, they've got it. But it's not that. You then have to merge yourself with the target. So you're not separate. The whole point is to be connected to the target."

Really?

"All great golf performances come out of a state of being connected to the target. All great players have experienced that. Afterward they think, 'What was that? There's something mystical about it.' There's some new research that's proven that when golfers give their best performances their EEGs are in an easy, regular pattern, an alpha state. Then when they make a bad shot, their EEGs go all erratic, and things go downhill from there. So we know that when players are playing their best golf their hearts are relaxed and, I would say, open. People play golf to keep re-creating that experience. For the moment, when you hit that shot, you didn't get in your own way. We call it 'Heart Golf'—the science behind it is staggering. I like to think of golf as 'Greater Optimal Life Focus.' "

Heart Golf! Could that explain why I'd hit so well when I felt like I was falling in love with Graham? My heart was open!?

"Absolutely," Lynn confirmed. "The trick is to stay in that heart space all the time. Nancy's a great example. She does that a lot. People know when other people are in that state, and they're attracted to it, because it's a glimpse of what they could do. And she has such an incredible following. People love to watch her play. Nancy is it, with women's golf. She's a Heart Golf guide."

When I returned to my hotel room I spotted someone who looked a lot like Nancy Lopez walking around the parking lot carrying a foil-covered casserole dish. She looked up and waved.

"Do you have a kitchen?" she called up.

I did.

Nancy was up the stairs in a flash . . . a flash of aluminum. Moments later her chicken casserole was baking in my oven. Moments after that I was in her kitchen, watching her make baked beans and sweet iced tea, Georgia style.

We talked about all sorts of things. About how she doesn't think about anything when she's taking a swing. And how putting is "all feel," and how if you don't see the ball go in the hole, you start missing. About how good she was when she was younger because she putted "by instinct." About how she juggles raising her girls with daily golf practice. About how Pebble Beach is the most beautiful golf course she's ever played. And how playing in England was the "most fun." And how her favorite U.S. course on the tour is Wykagyl Country Club in New Rochelle, New York: "It suits my personality. It's long, it's tough, the greens are not real big."

Then I asked her if she ever dreams about golf. Nancy stopped cooking and looked at me purposefully.

"I only have one golf dream," she said. "And it's always the same one."

She cleared her throat.

"I always say if I have a backswing—no matter how much trouble I get in—I still have a shot. No matter how much trouble you're in, if you can take the club back, you're okay. So, I have this dream that I'm on a tee—I'm not sure which tee it is—and I tee the ball up, and I go to take a swing and there's a tree in my backswing. It's always the same tee, always a tree. My whole theory of golf is if you still have a backswing, you still have a shot . . ."

"And in this dream, you don't have a shot?"

"It's more of a nightmare."

"Well, it means something," I told her. "There's something there. I can feel it."

"Um-hmm," Nancy agreed. "But I don't know what."

The following morning Nancy graciously gave me a quick golf lesson on the lawn behind her hotel room. It had rained during the night, and the morning was washed lilac. Birds sang at a fever pitch and the air smelled like the desert.

Nancy checked my grip. Then she suggested that I point my toes "outward."

"If your toes are pointed outward you have a better extension toward your target. But if they're closed, then you're blocking."

Blocking. Great. Something else to think about.

"So keep your knees flexed and relaxed. Just be as natural as you can. That's what you want to do. Your grip looks great!"

I confess to extreme satisfaction in hearing Nancy Lopez voice approval of *my* golf grip. Jeez.

"Okay, now you were taking everything back with your turn. You don't want to do that. You want to keep your lower body pretty still, and you want to turn at your waist. Keep your hips more still. There you go. And the most important thing is, when you take the club back, keep your eye on the back of the ball. So, when you take your club back, your eye's still on the ball, still on the ball, still on the ball . . . on the *back* of the ball, then when you hit it you follow through to your target. There you go.

"And the big thing for women, you gotta tell 'em to swing hard. As in, kill it. Put somebody's name on the ball who you don't like a lot. Just think of somebody. Put their name on the ball, then you just whack it. There you go, that was more aggressive. You're going to play your best golf when you're aggressive. Oooh, that was good. Real good. Keep those knees flexed. Yeah, that's good. Now, be sure your knees are flexed *all* the way through the ball. There you go. That's good."

I took an aggressive swing and removed a sizeable swath of lawn.

"Oh no!"

"That's okay," Nancy said, giggling. "You want to take divots. My dad always told me, '*Dig!*' You should go to the driving range. If you like to listen to music, take a headset and listen while you practice."

"What kind of music do you listen to while you practice?"

"I like Kenny G. Something instrumental. Now, eventually, after you've hit enough shots, you'll know what they're supposed to feel like. So you kind of feel yourself into learning. I taught myself lots of shots. I played in a different way. But it works."

I asked her to show me.

"Okay, now I like to keep it simple. And keep it slow. I like to keep my knees flexed. Takin' it back too quickly is not good. So I take it back slow, keeping my hips still, turning the body, then when I come through I keep my eyes behind the ball, then follow through."

A flawless, beauteous shot.

"I think women are sometimes intimidated because they think they should swing like a woman," Nancy ventured. "You want to swing like an athlete. Not like a man, like an athlete. But your swing looks real good. How long have you played?"

"Not quite a year yet."

"You should go out for a week and just hit golf balls. Because the big thing in golf is not how far you hit it, but how straight. 'Cause you don't want to get in trouble."

Trouble. The Tree In Her Dream. I told her I'd been thinking about that tree. And I said that I had a powerful feeling that it represented *some*thing that was blocking her, some emotional thing. She nodded. "A fear of failure, probably," she said.

I nodded. Then I told her my sister said she'd be happy to do a hypnosis session on her dream if she was interested.

Nancy Lopez nodded. And smiled. And said she was.

16

....

gentlemen only, ladies forbidden

The sky was the color of haggis. The air was clabbered with cold. A north wind made little hair tornadoes on top of our heads, and yellow leaves stuck to our faces like weather tattoos. Autumn was coming, and all I could think about was how much Scotland smelled like Oregon.

Seonaid McAinsh had taken a bus to meet my plane in Edinburgh so that we could drive back to St Andrews together. But first we had to make it to my rental car alive. Seonaid drilled her fists into her jacket pockets and hunched her shoulders against the wind, which had already rouged her cheeks a vibrant magenta. She had the habit of turning and taking gliding sidesteps while walking, which gave you the vague sense of being in a soccer game. And she spoke with the kind of animation usually reserved for dinner tables and pubs. Seonaid McAinsh did not seem like a woman recovering from surgery.

"Yoo know," she was saying, "the women set up all theese gowlf clubs for themselves rrrrather than make a'cood'searrr of it."

"A what?"

"A cod's ear," she repeated, trying to air out her dense Glasgow accent. "You know, a bourrechie."

"A *who*?"

"A bourr-a-hee. A jumble. A mess. It would'a beeen a rrreal mess if they had'a gone ta fight tha men ov'r bein' in their gowlf clubs, now, woulddaan't-hit?"

It was hard to believe she was speaking English. I suspected problems with my ears after the long flight. Or maybe airport food poisoning.

"Can you get Mad Cow disease from a hot dog?" I asked her.

"No," said Seonaid. "But you kin go barkin' mad."

"All rrright," she began, once we were on the highway, "firrrst we'rre going ta stop by the Lundin Ladies Gowlf Club."

"We have to go all the way back to London??"

"No, it's L-u-n-d-i-n, in the town o' Lower Larrrgo, birrrth-place o' Rrrrobinson Crrrusoe. It's on the way'ta St Andrews."

What a relief. I'd just come from London . . . via Los Angeles. Actually, I didn't feel as bad as I should have because somehow Graham had arranged for me to fly "upper class" on Virgin Atlantic Airways, the glamorously hip airline to the stars. It was easy to see why they choose it. First of all, I actually *slept* during most of the overnight flight, in my own cool little one-piece "Snooze Suit" on a seat that virtually became a futon. Before that I'd been treated to what had amounted to haute spa cuisine, a bottomless glass of Evian and just the right number of European chocolates. Before we landed, an onboard esthetician gave me a shoulder massage and a hand reflexology treatment that included "working" my "jet lag points." I'd even been able to practice my short game on the putting green in the Virgin Atlantic Clubhouse at Heathrow Airport. All of which allowed me to be coherent enough to focus at the Lundin Ladies Golf Club after flying five thousand miles nonstop against the turn of the earth.

The Lundin Ladies club was our first stop on the grand Scottish women's golf tour Seonaid had graciously planned for us. And a historic collection it was. Nearly all of the eight clubs on her list had been founded more than a century ago: the Ladies' Putting Club of St Andrews in 1867; the Carnoustie Ladies' Golf Club in 1873; the Ladies' Golf Club, Troon, in 1882; the Lundin Ladies Golf Club in 1891; the Aberdeen Ladies Golf Club in 1892; the St Rule Club in 1898; the Gullane Ladies' Golf Club in 1904; and the St Regulus Ladies' Golf Club in 1913.

"Lundin Ladies is the only club that still owns its own golf courrrse," Seonaid informed me, a fact that appeared to be a well-guarded secret. Even she had trouble locating the cobbled side street that magically opened onto an unexpected sweep of green behind a long row of pretty, old stone houses. The Lundin Ladies course, I soon learned, featured eighteen holes of natural golf. It wasn't played on links land, as I had imagined all golf courses in Scotland were, but on authentic Scottish countryside made painterly by glens and dales, Robin Hood trees, and mysterious ancient standing stones, all beneath a lowering Celtic sky.

The club parking lot was tucked in betwixt private residences and a one-story clubhouse that faced the 18th green. As I took in its welcoming, unassuming appearance, two welcoming, unassuming apple-cheeked golfers approached. They were Sigrid Henderson and the startlingly named Helen Bunker. Both were, they told us, pleased to have managed to play nine holes in the recent "blink of sun."

"We were lucky," Helen said gratefully. "It looks like it will rain, but it hasn't."

"So you're visitin'," Sigrid began. "Well, you've got to see the standing stones."

"And then there's the burn at the seventh and ninth," Helen added.

"You've had a *fire*?" I asked.

"A burrn is a wee riverrr," Seonaid told me. "A strream."

The wind suddenly intensified.

"You must be chilled," Helen said.

"Go inside the clubhouse," Sigrid offered. "It's warmer, and there's a kettle for tea and coffee."

"Here, I'll show you," Helen added, leading the way.

The Lundin Ladies' clubhouse was a cottage, really, modest, well cared for, prim with new paint. Inside it felt more like a home than a clubhouse, the result, I'm sure, of belonging to women. Its kitchen was small and spotless. A "Foxes Assortment" biscuit tin sitting on the counter revealed two homemade scones. A sign reminded you to pay your 20 pence for coffee or tea. On the wall I saw a note that I found oddly touching:

> I always like to look my best,
> For members, friends, and all my guests,
> So tidy up before you leave me,
> And I'll be happy to receive thee!
>
>   Your Kitchen

Nearby, also on the wall, there were instructions regarding a certain "Fire blanket for kitchen and clothing fires." It was illustrated by an alarming drawing of a woman lying on the floor, wrapped up in what looked like a roll of linoleum, her ankles and high heels sticking out of one end, her head sticking out of the other. I plugged in the electric teakettle with extravagant care.

The clubhouse bathroom and locker room were equally cheery, both fitted with smart new pine trim. The floor of the main room was inlaid with an artful mandala of a female form swinging a golf club and encircled by the words "Lundin Ladies Golf Club, Est. 1891." And hanging by itself on the wall to the right was a modestly framed handwritten note that read:

> February 27/08
> Ladies house proprietarie now-1909 to move the
> present clubhouse to new ground—
> rental

Say east field 12 acres
@ 2 of £12
Stan'dq [that's exactly how it was spelled] *Stone field 14 acres*
@ £29   £17.10
                     £29.10

It commemorated the day the Lundin Ladies became the proud owners of their own land.

"This rrroute is the way the pilgrims used to come to visit the bones of St Andrews in the eleventh and twelfth century," Seonaid announced as we continued our drive north. "But the only bit of him that was left was his forearm."

"Are they sure it's his?"

"Of course not," Seonaid snapped. "But they're sure it's a forearm."

"That's appropriate for the home of golf," I replied. Hearing the term "home of golf" spoken out loud, even by myself, made me happy. The late hour had inspired us to forgo a tour of the Lundin Ladies' golf course proper and push on to St Andrews. My resulting excitement as experienced through the morphinelike fog of descending jet lag carried a mystical charge. But then a visit to any mecca is a spiritual event. Graham was right. I couldn't wait to see St Andrews in person—hear it, smell it, put my hand in the hand, as it were. And I couldn't help but wonder how on earth a little seaside desert of sand, heather, and thorny whin, built upon a rocky, wind-thrashed peninsula pointing due east into the furious North Sea, could have given the world something as dependent on inward serenity as the game of golf.

Without Seonaid, the thrill of approaching St Andrews would have been unbearable . . . I would have been driving. Being directionally dyslexic, driving in a country where both the position of the driver and the direction of traffic are reversed from what I'm used to, would not have been my idea of a vacation. Thus had Seonaid become our designated driver. Besides, she knew the place.

By 6:45 that evening—God knows what hour in Oregon Time—Seonaid waved a hand toward the windshield.

"The lights o' St Andrews," she announced. "An' therre's no brrilliant way to get there."

Indeed, our route zigged and zagged until Seonaid was, at last, threading our rented Saab through the ancient streets of St Andrews. Finally we pulled into a parking lot as hidden as the Lundin Ladies' golf course had been. Seonaid led us around a corner and down a pretty little walking lane that ran between two sides of backyards.

"Lede Braes," she declared.

"For good weather?" I asked, assuming she was invoking divine intervention.

Seonaid frowned.

"*What?*"

"Didn't you say, 'Let us pray'?"

"Naow!" she replied. "I said 'lead-dee brays' . . . as in L-e-d-e B-r-a-e-s. Tha's the name o' th' lane. The mill riverr used t'rrun here. It used t'be a wee channeled burrn."

I wanted to come back with something about walking on water, but didn't dare.

Seonaid led us down the charming Lede Braes to an equally charming gate and steps, then a garden, then a house, which I soon learned was the home of her neighbor, fellow physical education teacher, women's golf aficionado, and best pal Frances Humphries.

Frances was waiting for us. A small, tightly wound woman with searching, compassionate eyes, she moved with a velocity that made Seonaid seem positively languid. During one long, run-on sentence, Frances led me upstairs, showed me my pretty room with its grand view of many ancient roofs, showed me my bathroom, showed me how the tricky European shower worked, led me back downstairs, showed me how the heating system worked, showed me how the electric teakettle worked, showed me the tea, showed me the breakfast cereals, pointed out the fruit bowl full of apples, bananas, and oranges, showed me the refrigerator freshly stocked with eggs, sausage, cheese, bread, and milk, showed me the phone in her study and how to make overseas calls, then informed me that the house was mine for my entire visit . . . She'd be down the lane at Seonaid's if I needed anything.

Such is the dedication of Scottish women golfers to seekers of the history of women's golf. I owed my Scottish golf contact, Archie Baird, a very serious thank-you.

I have lived in Europe, and visited many times, but the elemental beauty of its old stone villages never ceases to move me. St Andrews certainly is one of Europe's finest. Its buildings are some of the oldest in Scotland, and the most architecturally diverse. You might take tea in a perfect example of Gothic architecture, peruse single-malt whiskeys in Greek or Georgian, pass through a medieval archway to buy souvenir golf balls for your hometown golf coach—whose father, in Al Mundle's case, once attended St Andrews University, which, in 1853, founded the world's first university golf club. The town remains a wondrous grid of long, narrow streets filled with talkative students and fast-walking residents darting birdlike in and out of the little shops Americans love. St Andrews, most definitely, is a village lover's village.

And Seonaid's 1830 stone cottage is a cottage lover's cottage. Rested and happy, the next morning I made the half-minute walk down Lede Braes from Frances's house to Seonaid's garden gate, sipping in the early mist as I went, eventually figured out the gate's deceptively simple latch, and arrived at her back door having threaded through a backyard as natural and well planted as Frances's front yard was. Once inside I found both my Scottish golf coaches sitting at Seonaid's kitchen table staring at what appeared to be a very old, slightly bruised, softball-sized golf ball.

"Well, that's what we were goin' ta tell ya 'twas," Seonaid confessed. "But, rreally 'tis a fresh haggis Frances went out an' bought fer us."

I soon learned that haggis is to the culinary arts what The Yips are to golf. Most people seem to be allergic to it (including Frances, who announced with a strongly turned down mouth that she "never cared for it"), nobody will tell you what it really is, and, in Scotland anyway, it's here to stay. This last fact is unfortunate. Haggis seems to be more than remotely associated with sheep's guts, and, in reality, amounts to a sort of light *Braveheart* snack food terminally unsuited for modern Western palates accustomed to California roll and Pad Thai. Personally, I would just as soon have considered the haggis an obsolete golf ball and left it at that. To that end, I made grand Boy-am-I-full! belly-patting gestures, complimented Frances on her wide selection of breakfast cereals, implied that I'd sampled them all, each with all of the species of fruit she'd provided, then cooked up some scrambled eggs and toast and finished it all off with multiple cups of tea. The haggis, much to my (and I believe Frances's) relief, was retired to Seonaid's refrigerator, and we were, at last, off on our continuing girl golf tour. Frances insisted on remaining behind, I assumed to discreetly dispose of the horrifying haggis in our absence, perhaps as a treat for Juma, Seonaid's cocker spaniel, whose previous owner was a renowned St Andrews character and fine woman golfer who, while working in India, had won the North of India Golf Championship. Even my golf guide's dog had a golfing pedigree!

"This is the Royal and Ancient," Seonaid declared, waving her cigarette in the direction of the famed many-columned clubhouse. I couldn't help but stare. Not only because of the building's classic beauty, but because it houses the most exclusive golf club on earth and governing body for the entire world of golf. It is within the revered walls of the Royal and Ancient Club (R&A), for instance, that the allowable number of golf ball dimples on any new design is decided. Or the angle of a new club head. Or any ruling disagreement, including, I hoped, whether a golfer should be allowed on a golf course without brushing his teeth after a luncheon of haggis.

"And yoo know," Seonaid offered, "women arrn't allowed inside except on one day a yearr at the end o' November.

"Now this is the eighteenth green of the Old Course," she continued as we walked along the narrow cobbled road that fronts the row of stone buildings facing the course's 18th fairway. "No women are allowed there, either."

"So, where do you and Frances usually play?" I asked.

"The Jubilee Course, o' course," Seonaid answered.

I should have known. The Jubilee Course had been built in 1897 in honor of Queen Victoria's Diamond Jubilee, and when it was completed it was immediately nicknamed the Ladies' Course. But unlike the Old Course, its holes had never been named. For its centenary in 1997, a hole-naming competition had been held, and two of Frances's entries had won.

"I had suggested they name the fifth hole 'Hacky's Barra,'" Frances had explained. "A barra is a barrow, like your wheelbarrow. Hacky was a simpleton, a local character. He had hardly any education and he was taken in by the owners o' Henderson's Book Shop on Church Street. He lived with the couple for years—he had no family. He swept the floor and they gave him a barrow to make deliveries with, even if just a letter. When I saw the shape o' the fifth hole it reminded me of a barra, an' I thought, 'Hackey!'"

Frances named the Jubilee's 17th hole "Ladyhead" after "the area where the fisherfolk all lived," she told me. "I just plucked that out of thin air, because the fisherfolk often caddied when they weren't out at sea."

"The funniest thing was that it came to the last week and none of mine had been accepted," Seonaid told me. "An' as we were walkin' to post her names Frances said, 'I've already won a hole so I'll give you a couple of my names.' But I refused her offer and put in me own names. And after we posted her names, a seagull did a great big whoopsie on top o' Frances— on her head and down her back. An' I said, 'That's good luck!' An' she won the second hole, an' I got nothin' again.

"Now, women *are* allowed on the Old Course on Sundays to lay out the laundry," Seonaid said. "Speakin' o' clothes," she added, "the St Andrews Woollen Mill here is goin' out o' business and havin' a mighty sale—yoo might take a wee glance."

Now, there was a statement with "Christmas shopping" written all over it. In the store's well-worn, decidedly un-modern aisles I found handsome men's golf sweaters whose St Andrews Woollen Mill labels alone were worth their thrice-reduced $25 price tags. There were also Loch Ness monster kids' T-shirts for Jesse and my nuclear niece, Amber, and, joy of joys, *the* answer to my bedeviling women's golf clothes problem: authentic Scottish minikilts! In a handsome dark green-on-navy Black Watch tartan with cute little buckle front-flap fasteners. That took care of my own St Andrews souvenir as well as Candace's . . . except for one small problem: the size. The fitting room revealed a vanity disas-ter—in kilts we wore a 12, not a 6!

I was pleased to learn from the mill's sympathetic sales-women that this was the product of peculiar Scottish sizing, not porridge poisoning. Still, it presented a problem worthy of a Royal and Ancient ruling: Do you remove the authentic St Andrews Woollen Mill label in order to destroy size evi-dence? Or do you leave things intact and set your girl golf buddy up for endlessly embarrassing locker room dis-claimers? I went with the disclaimers . . . and perhaps a pre-Christmas session with a Magic Marker.

Page 217

Three shopping bags later, we stepped toward the front door and I glanced at the wall and noticed for the umpteenth time a black-and-white photo of the *same* bewhiskered gray-haired old man with the same startled look on his face. I'd seen the photo on shop walls all over town.

"Is he the saint of St Andrews or something?" I asked Seonaid.

"Yoo could say that," she replied. "That's Ol' Tom Morrris, the Grand Old Man o' Golf. He was a famous golfer—th' father o' Scottish golf, reeally. A golfing celebrity o' the firrst waterr."

"He fly fished, too?" I asked excitedly.

Seonaid eyed me sidelong.

"Naow, it's a figger o' speech. Firrst waterr . . . as in firrst level, top drrawer. Yoo know, th' best! An' he was a famous clubmaker. Won fourr St Andrrews Golf Club National Championships, in 1861, '62, '64, an' '67. His son Young Tom Morrris won four in a rrow . . . then he lost his firstborn and young wife in childbirth, an' died himself soon after."

Seonaid looked away. Then brightened and nodded at something up ahead.

"An' there's our famous Swilcan Bridge way down therre on the Swilcan Burn . . . strrream to yoo. Eight hundred yearrs old."

It was a handsome, squat old stone thing.

"Everryone who's anyone in golf has passed over it on theirr way down the last fairrway here—we call this the Tom Morrrris Hole. An' therre's the Valley of Sin," she added, waving to a horrific bunker precisely in front of the green. "The secret t'playin' the hole is t'line up with the clock on the Royal an' Ancient Clubhouse."

Of course.

Ah, the purity of it! Golf wasn't invented in St Andrews, but it became the game it is there. Originally a herdsman's game of staff and stone, a primitive Netherlands sport called

Het Kolven. A game for which the irregular seaside linksland of the Scottish coast was made. A game born of the wily boreal wind and everywhere gorse, a game fraught with endless unpredictability and variables, a game as chaotic as the human mind, as fractionated by moving parts as the human hand, a game that holds at its trickster heart the most addictive of psychological conditions: intermittent reward. In short, a game guaranteed to drive oneself crazy. And the secret to the 18th hole of the most famous golf course on earth is . . . a *clock*?

Perfect. How golflike. How just like golf.

That giddy dizziness was upon me again. I was either hyperventilating or breathing too deeply of the rarefied St Andrews air. I definitely had the golf vapors. Truly, I needed to sit down. As luck would have it, sitting down was next on the agenda. We had been invited to lunch at the elegant St Rule Club, the women's answer to the Royal and Ancient Club, housed in a classic Victorian townhouse on the Old Course's Links Road overlooking the hallowed 18th hole.

We were, it turned out, guests of Seonaid's friend, fellow physical education teacher and long-term St Rule member Joy Steele. Joy *was* joyful, a boyishly lean, elfin-eyed woman with an unintentionally chic coiffure of cropped pure white bed-head hair who finished each word with a startling clip that made her mercifully easy to understand. Seonaid simply pronounced Joy's accent "posh."

"We celebrated our centenary this year," Joy explained as we took seats near the bow window in St Rule's sun-flooded drawing room. "And since it's in the rules that women *can* lay out their laundry to dry on the Old Course on Sundays, we did just that as part of our celebration, dressed in authentic period clothes. Oh, the press loved it!"

Joy swiftly produced photos to prove it. The women of St Rule, long-skirted and behatted, crossing over Swilcan

Bridge with baskets of laundry on their hips. Their costumes looked wonderfully authentic. "Oh, but they *were* authentic!" Joy confirmed happily. Then she produced a little flyer explaining the club's history, as well as a book about the club titled *For the Good of Golf and St Andrews: The St Rule Club,* by Marcia Ellen Julius (an American!), published in honor of the club's 1998 centenary celebration.

It was hardly a surprise to learn that St Rule was founded as an "exclusive club for wealthy and well-connected ladies," but I was fascinated by the lifestyle of these women a hundred years ago. Many of them, for instance, had husbands who were living and working abroad in the colonial service. Often a woman would be separated from her husband for years. If she lived out of town, a trip to town via horse and carriage was an all-day ordeal.

"Once a lady was in St Andrews, there were shops, and you could have luncheon or tea," reports St Andrews historian Marjorie Moncrieff, "but that was it. There was nothing else."

It was easy to see why Joy's flyer listed the first purpose of the St Rule Club as "social," not "golf." In fact, all of St Rule's original purposes were social. Members were "to share newspapers and periodicals," "to have tea and light refreshments," and "to have a shelter near the links." I was amazed to learn that a women's social club wasn't a woman's idea, it was a man's—Royal and Ancient Club member Captain George M. Boothby. In fact, most St Rule members' husbands were and are members of the R&A, who to this day are allowed to become associate members of St Rule. "Of course," Joy's book assured us, "there was absolutely no mention of the fair sex in the R&A rules."

Of course.

Nonetheless, a women's club in conservative St Andrews challenged the status quo. After the St Rule Club was founded, a local newspaper columnist wrote that after the man of the house "stays late and pleads that he has been detained by jolly company at the Club, the next night the woman of the house will be able to say, 'Oh, I have had such an exciting game at my Club . . . and could not get home a moment sooner. Club life, dear, is so nice.'"

"It was," declares Marcia Julius, "the seal of approval from the Victorian male establishment!"

But what, I wanted to know, did all this have to do with women's golf? After all, by the time the St Rule Club was founded, the Ladies' Golf Union had been going strong for five years, the British Amateur Ladies' Championship had been established for four, and five women's golf clubs were already in existence, including the Lundin Ladies. The world-famous Ladies' Putting Club of St Andrews had glorified women's short game for better than three decades!

As it turned out, it only took two general meetings of the St Rule Club for someone to move that a St Rule Golf Club be formed. It was. The clubs merged in 1952 under the general St Rule name, and today there is a waiting list to get in.

"However," Joy confessed, "five spaces are kept open for golfers with low handicaps, and two hundred sixty-three of our four ninety-five total are golfing members who pay subscriptions to the Ladies' Golf Union."

There were also, I noted, twenty-seven male associate members.

In 1903, members of St Rule helped organize the first Scottish Ladies Golf Championship. Now, each May, the club sponsors one of the leading amateur tournaments in women's golf, the international St Rule Trophy. But one need only step downstairs to see the real prize of the St Rule Club—its Golf Room, an orderly, beautifully be-lockered tribute to Scottish women and golf. The grand feeling of the place surely has something to do with the fact that it is the former workshop of good Old Tom Morris.

"Yoo can see here," Joy said, pointing to the flyer, "that we were able to take over the ground floor of this building in 1906. It had belonged to Tom Morris Clubmakers," she added with obvious pride.

"And yoo know," Seonaid confided, once we had said our thank-yous and good-byes and were walking again along the Links Road, "Joy herself is a crack golfer."

That night we dined in the back room of the Dunvegan Hotel in downtown St Andrews. The only other diners were a dozen Royal and Ancient Club members seated at the table behind ours. There was much discussion about a man who had shot a 76 on the Old Course recently, then changed it to a 72. "The Captain maintains that he'd done it before," a gentleman reported, his jowls quivering with consternation. "Turns out, he has a young wife who's better than he is. Apparently, he keeps trying to impress her."

"Robin, it *says* 'the lock closest to the sea.' Now, that has to be *this* one."

With the afternoon had come the wind, and Seonaid and I found ourselves huddled on the south side of the very locked-up clubhouse of the Ladies' Putting Club of St Andrews. To our left, the North Sea billowed with whitecaps— or white horses, as the Scots call them. To our far right lay the narrow throat of the Old Course. Closer in, just in front of the clubhouse, the Ladies' astonishingly hilly eighteen-hole putting green soared and dipped like the Himalayas— which is the course's nickname. Its swales are, in fact, natural sand dunes that today were sans holes or pins, since the course and its clubhouse were closed for the winter.

Nonetheless, with characteristic good cheer, the club president, Muriel Davidson, had agreed to give us a tour.

"I had a great time telling Sean Connery to get off the putting green once," she said as longtime member Enid Wilson tried all four keys in all six locks near to and far from the sea on all three of the clubhouse's side doors. "Of course, I didn't know it was he," Muriel added. "Did you know he's a member of the Royal and Ancient?"

To make Enid's task ever more challenging, all the doors were blocked by a heavy wooden bench. Trying to be helpful, Enid's husband, Robert—whom the women called Robin— moved the bench. Enid yelped.

"Not while I'm *working!*" she cried.

But a mischievous smile gave her away. Enid was a bit of a Scottish drama queen.

Finally, Seonaid scaled the front gate, managed to unlock the front door, and let us all in from inside.

Founded in 1867, the Ladies' Putting Club had recently renovated its clubhouse, much to everyone's approval. Venerated golf historian Marjorie Moncrieff contends that it was the addition of a telephone in 1969 that "really brought the club back to life," allowing for game planning and checking on family at home. On the wall above the phone hung a photo of George Bush putting with a two-handed under-the-chin putter, "I loved playing your very special course" scrawled across a corner.

"We've even got a dishwasher!" Enid crowed happily. "It's cozy now."

Still, unlike the refined parlor atmosphere of St Rule, the Ladies' Putting Club clubhouse has the feel of a place far more businesslike than social.

"We have more than two hundred members, and most take their putting very seriously," Muriel assured. "We play often."

Nearby, a small side room was lined with rental putters and golf balls, stored by color in egg cartons—some fifty thousand visitors play the course each season.

In the early days, according to Marjorie Moncrieff, "a competition was a tremendous social occasion. At its biggest we had four hundred women members, two hundred men. When a top woman lost she was *very* upset."

"Old Tom Morris was our first groundskeeper," Robin added in a voice so slow and deep it sounded as if it had rolled out of the bowels of the Royal and Ancient Clubhouse more than a full block away. I literally jumped. "Today the groundskeeper still changes the holes every week, sometimes twice a week."

When asked just how the holes were changed, Robin vanished and reappeared with a medieval-looking metal hole-cutting device. As he began to demonstrate, Enid yelped again.

"You'll cut a hole in the carpet!" she wailed. Then smiled.

"We have putting handicaps," Muriel went on. "The best is plus five. We have a number of competitions. Started the Victoria Jubilee Plate in 1886, for instance. Our trophies are kept in the bank and never come out."

"A few can go home," Enid corrected. "I've got one of them—it's for the best of the worst." She smiled. "We play St Rule and St Regulus."

"I'm a member of St Regulus," Seonaid offered.

"Oh, they do so much good work," Muriel replied.

"We also play the past captains of the Royal and Ancient," Enid added, rolling her eyes. "The *men*."

"We *won* this year," Muriel pointed out.

"Mrs. Davidson's Putter of the Year," Enid announced. "The trophy's a Silver Putter, sits in a case."

"In the bank." Muriel sighed.

Enid yelped again. She had tripped on something invisible.

"Men can be associate members," Muriel explained. "Robin's one of our best putters."

It didn't take much to talk them into an indoor putting match.

"All right, then, between the table legs," Robin began.

On top of the table sat the president's gavel—a wooden shaft with a genuine antique rubber gutta golf ball attached to the end.

"The arrrival of the cheaperr gutta ball is what made the common man be able t'afford t'play, ya know," Seonaid informed me. "Beforre that they only had th' featherie—a leatherr ball stuffed all full o' featherrs. Cost a bloody forrtune."

I considered that portentous bit of history as Muriel took her position on the opposite side of the room. When I turned to watch, I was surprised to catch a distinctly predatory gleam in her eyes. She lined up, looked again, and putted. Her line, to plagiarize Cherry Gillespie, was surgical. Her ball followed obediently. A perfect putt. Between the table legs without touching either.

Robin took Muriel's place. He lined up. He cocked his head and his eyes narrowed. At the exact moment he putted, Enid yelped again. A tumbler of pencils had somehow fallen off a desk. Enid smiled. Apparently Robin was immune to his wife's influences—his putt was as deadly as Muriel's. It was a draw.

Both contestants seemed pleased.

"Putting is a feel, a touch," Muriel told us. "I was putting since I was this high. We practiced on the carpet."

"It's the way you take it back," Robin said. "You have to get the wrist firm."

"The flat bit is the true test of putting," Muriel concluded.

For members of the Ladies' Putting Club of St Andrews, three-foot swales, apparently, are the easy part.

The second morning bloomed clear and cold. A perfect travel day. But by the time we arrived at Scotland's famed Royal Troon Golf Club we were in haggis weather again. To the west, a trio of Quasimodo guy golfers strode down Royal

Troon's 17th fairway hunched dramatically against the rain. Beyond them the rock island of Ailsa Craig rose sea serpent—like in the misted Firth of Clyde.

"I'm Sheila Ness," the woman said brightly, "like the monster. I'm our handicap and golf convenor. This is Louise Huchinson, our house convenor. And this," Mrs. Ness concluded with obvious pride, "is Margaret Sharp, our 1998–99 captain."

With golfers' handshakes, they welcomed us to the handsome, surprisingly spacious Victorian clubhouse of the Ladies' Golf Club, Troon.

The beautiful clubhouse was built in 1897, fifteen years after the club itself was founded, and fully three centuries after Mary, Queen of Scots, had taken so keenly to golf that when her husband died she only waited six days to play another round. "She should at least have waited a week," the Scottish evangelist John Knox had supposedly grumbled.

As I was swiftly learning, Scottish women have been serious about the game from the start. But when a golfer thinks of Troon or Aberdeen, Carnoustie, Gullane, or the sacred playing grounds of St Andrews, "women's golf" is not the term that comes to mind. Laura Davies and Nancy Lopez aside, the truth is that men generally have not welcomed women into the royal and ancient game.

"I thought you might like to see this," offered Captain Sharp as she thrust forth a copy of a letter dated 9th April, 1893, and sent to "Miss Martin" by Horace Hutchinson, then a leading British golf amateur. It read:

I have read your letter about the proposed Ladies' Golf Union with much interest. Let me give you the famous advice of Mr Punch . . . DON'T. My reasons? Well!

1. Women never have and never can unite to push any scheme to success. They are bound to fall out and quarrel on the smallest or no provocation; they are built that way!

2. They will never go through one Ladies' Championship credit. Tears will bedew, if wigs do not bestrew, the green.

3. Constitutionally and physically women are unfitted for golf. They will never last through two rounds of a long course in a day. Nor can they ever hope to defy the wind and weather encountered on our best links even in spring and summer. Temperamentally the strain will be too great for them. THE FIRST LADIES' CHAMPIONSHIP WILL BE THE LAST . . .

"Of course," Captain Sharp concluded sharply, "the first British Women's Championship was held three months later and has been going strong ever since."

So has Scottish women's golf. But what struck me standing there in the polished halls of the Troon Ladies' Golf Club was the dignity of it all. Rather than fight men for membership in *their* private clubs, Scottish women simply created their own . . . their own clubs, and clubhouses with their own captains, secretaries, lots of convenors, treasurers, budgets, restaurants and chefs, even bars, competitions, elaborate trophies, and in a few cases their own golf courses. I realized how lucky I was that Graham had arranged for me to come to Scotland to see it all for myself. The Troon Ladies' clubhouse was superlative. Beautifully built and maintained, it was graced with fine woodwork, a spotless locker area, and a light-filled upstairs dining room from which a kitchen staffer delivered us a tray of tea and the most wonderful homemade cookies, classic shortbread layered with jam.

"Those are our Empire Biscuits," Captain Sharp informed me with pride. "Would you like the recipe?"

A small piece of paper soon appeared bearing the names of only three ingredients and the lightest of directions. They were:

....

LADIES' GOLF CLUB, TROON

Empire Biscuits

1 lb. plain flour
10 oz. Soft butter
4 oz. Caster sugar

Cook in moderate oven until light
golden brown. When cold sandwich
together with jam and ice top.

....

Would that my golf swing were so elegant and winning.

The Troon Ladies' clubhouse included a very beautiful bar with a full selection of equally grand Scottish single-malt whiskeys. Seonaid wasted no time ordering us a "wee nip" of Dalwhinnie, a single-Highland-malt scotch whiskey made with spring water from the ancient Grampian Mountains. It smelled to me of honey and smoke, a perfume so intense and natural I wanted to dab some behind my ears. The Troon Ladies' young woman barkeep let me examine the bottle.

"Look, Seonaid," I said, "this is a special centenary edition. The Dalwhinnie distillery was founded in 1898, the same year the St Rule Club was."

"I'll drrink t'that!" Seonaid replied.

"An' then so will I," echoed the supremely elderly elegantly dressed woman seated at the bar a few stools down from us. "It's almost time for my *own* centenary, too!" Her enthusiasm so surprised us that both Seonaid and I laughed.

"To the well-aged whiskey an' the well-aged golferrr!" Seonaid toasted.

"To Scotland!" I replied.

"To gowlf!" added the elderly woman. "May it rrest in peace."

A full-on Scottish storm finally arrived while we headed north up the coast for Carnoustie and Aberdeen the next day. Icy monsoons lashed at the land and drove an opaque mist across the sea.

"Harr," Seonaid harrumphed.

As in disgruntled pirate?

"No, as in harr. A harr, spelt with two r's, is a type of heavy fog."

It was harrdly a day to receive golf visitors. Nonetheless, Robina Mathieson had the heater and the teakettle on for us at the Carnoustie Ladies' Golf Club clubhouse.

"My golf name is Robbie," she explained. "I'm vice captain and match secretary."

She's also a crack golf history buff. As Seonaid would say, "And, rrreally, not many people are."

Robina had prepared what she called a "potted history" of the club, meaning an abbreviated one, summed up in short takes of meeting minutes from the years 1873 until 1935. I noted some highlights: "July 1875: The 'Gold Medal' to be competed for annually was presented to the club. Also the silver monthly challenge medal." "July 1878: It was proposed to allow gentlemen associate members as the only means of keeping the club in existence. 38 gents were admitted." "July 1883: Gentlemen are reminded that as the course is exclusively for ladies they can only have the use of it when accompanied by ladies who are also playing." "June 1886: The club was now in a healthy state and the help of men was no longer needed." "August 26, 1895: The club house was opened."

And a lovely thing it still was, comforting and without guile, like the Lundin Ladies' clubhouse, a place in which any woman would feel very much at home.

Robina brought forth the Carnoustie Ladies' stunning collection of annual competition trophies—ornate, Victorian silver loving cups and chalices—then explained that the rectangle of lawn in front of the clubhouse used to be the ladies' putting green. Even more to the point, what is now Carnoustie's famed Burnside course was once the ladies' course. Over time, the Carnoustie Ladies lost their putting green and their golf course and are now allowed to play only at certain times on certain days. Still, Robina insisted that the women are "happy with things the way they are," a phrase echoed without exception at every women's golf club Seonaid and I visited. I can only assume the statement has its roots deep in the pride of ownership that each Scottish women's golf club offers each of its members.

Given the harr and the rain, it took forever to find Aberdeen. Passing farms looked drowned, their once-neat hay bales now soggy shredded wheat.

"It's grotty weather," Seonaid announced as we pulled into a gas station. She vanished into the station's convenience store and reappeared bearing twin bottles of Day-Glo orange soda.

"Irron Brew," she said, handing me one. "Made from garrters."

"How do they do that?"

"Do what?"

"Make drinks out of garters?"

"Girrrders," she repeated. "Like what holds up irron brridges. Full o' iron ferr yer blood."

"Well, I prefer All-One People," I said, and produced a small salmon-colored container from my day pack.

"I fearr to ask what *that* is made frroom," Seonaid said suspiciously.

"Oh, it's a powder that's got everything in it," I said. "Vitamins, minerals, trace minerals, antioxidants, enzymes . . . just stir it into juice. I won't travel without it."

"Well, yoo kin get all that in a good pint o' ale," she replied archly. "An' yoo don' have t'do any mixin' except with yer friends at the pub!"

Mightily amused at her own joke, Seonaid steered us back into the monsoon. Driving in it, whether in a car or off a tee, was next to impossible.

"So, do women actually play when it's like this?" I asked her.

"Oh, yeah," she said. "Or they jus' wait a wee bit 'til it clearrrs. Yoo know, like the men's Fruit Bowl."

"Hmmm . . . Fruit Bowl," I mused. "You'd think they'd call it the Haggis Bowl."

Seonaid frowned.

"Call what the *what*?"

I frowned.

"The Fruit Bowl. Like our Rose Bowl. But you have to admit," I added, observing the sheet rain that had turned the road into a water slide, "you don't exactly think of *fruit* when you think of Scotland."

Seonaid took her eyes off the road and regarded me for far longer than I felt was safe, given the driving conditions. Finally she spoke.

"Would ye like t'explain t'me just what on God's grreen earrth yer talkin' about?"

I did. Seonaid nodded.

"Well," she replied. "Yoo were close."

She had, in fact, said "football," having seen her share of

snow-blinded American defensive linemen running around television screens.

Due to the weather, we arrived late at the Aberdeen Ladies Golf Club clubhouse. Vice captain Midge Miller and honorary secretary Jennifer Risk were more than forgiving. Scottish women understand Scottish weather. As had Robina, they immediately offered us tea and sweets, served in the clubhouse's lovely heated solarium, a standing tribute to the stately era in which all Scottish women's golf clubs were born. The cookies looked delicious and I was dying to try one, but when Seonaid refused them I suspected some kind of golf club decorum and declined, comforting myself with the fact that the Aberdeen Ladies' tea was perfect.

The Aberdeen Ladies' whitewashed clubhouse was as well. It was as beautiful as it was Victorian. Its main room was still fitted with its founding members' curiously small wooden lockers. And its setting was magnificent. It was built on the greenest of flats, the geologic sinew of Royal Aberdeen linksland rolling sweetly to the sea before it. There was no traffic—there was hardly a hint of a road. It was like a precious, ornate cabin by the Scottish shore. I wanted to live there.

The Aberdeen women graciously presented us with a book about the club's history, published in 1992 for its centenary. A quick review revealed a passage that described the response of the men's club to the women's request for their own golf course:

THE CAPTAIN AND COUNCIL OF ABERDEEN GOLF CLUB MADE THREE STIPULATIONS: 1. THAT THE SUM OF 100 POUNDS BE PAID TO THE COUNCIL BY A.L.G.C. FOR LAYING OUT THE GROUND. 2. THAT THE LADIES SHOULD PROVIDE ACCOMMODATION FOR THEMSELVES ELSEWHERE THAN THE [MEN'S] CLUB

HOUSE. 3. THAT THE LADIES CLUB SHOULD HAVE
THE GROUND FOR SUCH TIME AS IT WAS NOT RE-
QUIRED FOR ANY PURPOSE OF THE ABERDEEN GOLF
CLUB. IT WAS ALSO TO BE RENT-FREE.

In other words, the women were to pay for building the
golf course, and could then use it until the men needed it for
something more important, as long as they also paid for
building their own clubhouse and didn't try to use the men's.

" 'Gentlemen Only, Ladies Forbidden,' " quoted Seonaid.
"Used t'be so many signs sayin' that on courrses all overr
Scotland that many people think that's wherre the worrd
'golf' came from. It isn't," she added. "But yoo know, it might
as well 'a been."

"There once *was* a sign on the front of the men's clubhouse that said all ladies were to use the rear entrance," reported vice captain Midge Miller. Her tone was the closest
anyone came to resentment during our entire tour. Except for
my own.

"Why weren't we allowed to eat the cookies?" I asked
Seonaid later.

"Well, yoo could'a have. An' why didn't yoo?"

"Because *you* didn't," I replied. "And neither did they, so I
assumed there was some sort of etiquette rule against it."

"Well, I just didn't fancy one, is all," she said. "Yoo could'a
eaten all yoo wanted!"

As they tend to do between the 44th and 45th Parallels, the
storm left the next day so polished it hurt your eyes to look at
it. Appropriate weather to meet the man responsible for my lu-
minous introduction to Scottish women's golf, Archie Baird.

A man of equally gleaming golf credentials, Archie had
married Dr. Sheila Park, great-granddaughter of Willie
Park, Sr., the first winner of the British Open Champi-

onship. After working as a veterinary surgeon for nearly three decades, Archie retired in 1980 and the same year opened the Heritage of Golf Museum at the Gullane Links, where golf has been played for more than three hundred years. Two years later he published a most charming and literary book, *Golf on Gullane Hill,* whose chapter titles alone would seduce any reader, with the possible exception of "Sheep's Head and Haggis," which, I was pleased to learn, referred not to a traditional golf food imposed upon visiting golfers but to the minutes of Gullane's first golf club, whose members, in 1888, requested that both dishes be provided at meetings. (They also asked that the whiskey and sherry decanters be changed so that they were "not quite so like each other as, after a certain period of the evening, some of the members found it very difficult to distinguish which was which.")

Archie was waiting for us. A muscular terrier of a man, he seemed to be in a hurry and wasted no time ushering us through the unmarked door of his modest, one-room golf museum adjacent to the Gullane pro shop.

"How do people find you here?" I asked him.

"They don't," he replied flatly. "They have to make an appointment . . . And we'll begin at the beginning," he began, "and the beginning was not in Scotland. The Dutch played a game like golf long before we did. There are enormous amounts of documentary and pictorial evidence to prove it, going back as far as 1400. There's no mention of golf in Scotland before 1450. BUT," he added, the word issuing forth from his mouth like rifle shot, "the Dutch neither developed the game nor did they keep it going. It died out totally in Holland by 1700. Because they couldn't make good clubs. They had no wood to make them with."

The Scots, on the other hand, had innumerable trees. And hills. And sheep. All of which, it turned out, had everything to do with why golf became a Scottish sport.

"You can't grow sheep on flat ground," Archie explained. "So our wool merchants took their wool to Holland, which was a very rich country, and sold it at a good price. And they had to wait for the wind to change to sail back."

Hence, they were introduced to and took up the Dutch game, which was played in the winter on frozen canals as far back as 1300, and one version of which was, indeed, called "colf."

"Is that where ice hockey came from, too?" I asked.

Archie frowned at me.

"It has nothing to do with hockey," he fairly spat. Then he produced a Dutch painting from 1668 called "Winter Sports (Kilted Figures playing golf.)."

"That guy and that guy are wearing kilts," Archie pointed out. "The Dutch never wore kilts."

So the Scots *did* golf in kilts! I was thrilled and about to say so when Archie, in rapid fire, added:

". . . BUT the Dutch *did* teach us how to make the feather ball. The feather ball came from Holland. Without a shadow of a doubt. A top hat full of feathers stuffed into a leather skin."

Archie plunked one into my hand, an authentic one, in mint condition, made before 1850. A true golfing treasure.

"And what will surprise you is how heavy it is," Archie added. He was right. It looked like an old, brown, smallish, seamed baseball, and had the weight of metal or wood.

"One of those sold in Edinburgh for twenty thousand pounds."

That was $40,000! I almost dropped the thing. Even in the beginning, a feather ball, or "featherie," cost as much as a golf club, which insured that golf remained a game for the rich.

"Until someone made a ball out of gutta-percha," Archie instructed, "and the game took off."

Gutta-percha—"gutta" for short, Archie explained—is a

tropical gum similar to rubber except that when it is heated it can be molded, and when it's cool it goes rock-hard. A gutta ball used to cost a tenth of a feather one.

"It was cheap and durable, not fragile and expensive," Archie said. "Now everyone could afford to play." To wit, in 1850 there were only fifteen golf courses in the world, but after the advent of the gutta ball, by 1900 there were twenty-three hundred.

In 1890, an American had invented the rubber core ball, which Archie pronounced "a nicer ball to hit, but a bouncy one. So they began to put all kinds of weird and wonderful markings on the face of clubs to try to put a bit of spin on the ball. Then another big change," Archie added, "was that they began to make club heads out of persimmon."

"Wouldn't that be a little . . . messy?" I ventured.

"Persimmon *wood*," Archie replied. "It's an American fruitwood and it is so hard you can bore a hole and stick a golf club shaft straight into it."

Archie proceeded to show us examples of antique golf clubs—"flanges, offset heads and oversized clubs . . . and that takes you up to the beginning of the steel shaft, where I lose interest."

There were antique ladies' hat pins that looked like little golf clubs, golf club–shaped buttonhooks, and a most amusing practice golf ball with its own parachute. There were early golf bags, including a charming wicker one from Hong Kong.

"Yoo could keep yer salmon in that, tooo," Seonaid offered.

"Lady Heathcoat-Amory could have really used it," I replied smugly.

Seonaid rose to the fly.

"Really?" she said. "And why woould tha' be?"

"Because after she won the British Women's Open at Troon in 1925, she went fishing in the Given River—"

"*Girvan,*" Seonaid corrected.

"Girvan River . . . and she got a twelve-pound salmon on her line, but she was so tired from playing all that golf that she told her fishing guide—"

"That woould be a *gillie,*" Seonaid interrupted.

". . . her gillie that she couldn't hold on. So he told her to pretend the salmon was the golfer who nearly beat her, somebody Leech . . ."

"*Cecil Leitch* . . . ," Seonaid supplied.

". . . okay, Leattchhh," I lisped back on purpose. "And she landed her fish!"

I had read the story in the sumptuous coffee table book the Ladies' Golf Union in St Andrews had sent me. Born Joyce Wethered, Lady Heathcoat-Amory was Scotland's star woman player in the 1920s, when she became the British champion four times, the English champion five times, and took the Curtis Cup in 1932. Of her auspicious fly fishing debut she herself wrote:

"And so golf and fishing unite in one delightful memory to remind one of the pleasures which no place in the world can supply in the same ample measure as Scotland."

"Auwk, well, maybe so," Archie allowed, "but we've got a tee time in five minutes, so the fishing kin wait."

The mystery of our rushed tour was solved; our guide hurried us out the museum door into a still bright sun. Which was when I saw them. Glowing like *objets sacrés* in the Gullane pro shop window: smart navy-blue and white British wing-tip women's golf shoes!

"Uh . . . just a minute, Archie," I said, much to his blustering, watch-watching chagrin. Minutes later I emerged reshod. I was ready, at last, to play Scotland.

We were to play a scramble. A fine player in her own right, Seonaid teamed up with Archie's longtime golf buddy, the wickedly accurate lanky shooter, Bill. Much to his misfortune, Archie was stuck with me.

Needless to say, I was a bundle of nerves. A well-heeled bundle of nerves, but a bundle of nerves nonetheless. I hovered over my first Scottish tee shot much as I had over my very first golf ball in Alabama. At least, this time the theme song to neither *Lawrence of Arabia* nor *Ozzie and Harriet* ran through my head. What ran through my head was much more serious than musings on the future of Western Civilization. What ran through my head was this: I am in the homeland of my ancestors, the homeland of golf, standing on Scottish soil, where the game has been played for three long centuries . . . and I am about to hit a *golf* ball.

"Well, *hit* it!" barked my partner.

I would have if I could have, but I couldn't, so I didn't.

There I was, my trusty Nancy Lopez driver in hand, my little Maxfli waiting patiently at my feet—"like a dog," I thought for some inexplicable reason—Archie waiting with palpable impatience not three feet away—"like a Scottish terrier," I realized, which clarified my earlier doggie-thought and brought an irrepressible smile to my lips. Which soon erupted into an air-leak giggle. Which spread, silver and jellyfish-like, around me, much as Virginia Woolf's headache. Except that there was no ache in it at all, and, frankly, not much head. What there was was heart. The astonishment of actually playing *golf* in Scotland had hit me full force, and suddenly my heart felt as wide as the Scottish linksland before me, as pure as the sky above.

And my heart took it all in, all of it: the sand and the bent grass and marram and moss, the fescue and silverweed and sea buckthorn and vetch, the foxes and partridges and roe deer and rabbits—the males of which, according to Archie, made golf's first holes by urinating in hollows on the links. Yes, my expanding heart took in rabbit pee-pee, too, scanning, as it did, up and down, to and fro, north, south, east, and west. I was in *Scotland*! Home of golf and birthplace of my very name, the only name I have answered to ever since

I could answer! The only one I've ever known. I am a *Maxwell,* a thousand years removed from Macus the Roman who, apparently, had a well somewhere down Dumfries way. A lowlander in the Highlands, I, but a Maxwell nonetheless. American clanswoman of Miss Annie Maxwell, the Scot who led the stroke competition in the Ladies' Championship at Gullane a century ago. A Maxwell, and a golfing one at that, anointed by Peggy Kirk Bell, mentored by Nancy Lopez, a Maxwell in my bones, whose very knees still carry my father's Scottish bump, which I used to pass off as a surfer's knob in my Boogie Board days, the bonnie bony bump, officially a tibial tuberosity, which evolved in Scottish warriors over the cold, northern millennia for extra muscle insertion, for battle, for extra *golf* power—no *wonder* I felt such a kinship with kilts! These knees are *supposed* to be bared to the wind! I am a Maxwell, I am, I am, and I am in *Scotland* and I am wearing a brand-new Scottish kilt and brand-new Scottish golf shoes and I, by God, am about to hit a Maxfli *golf* ball into the ancient Scottish wind . . . The prissy little French half of me had *no* choice but to sit down, fold her manicured little hands in her lap, and say, *"Oui, oui!"* I tried to expect nothing, but I knew I wanted *everything.* Van Morrison's imperfect perfect Celtic voice rose earnest and strong in my ears. *"Be Thou my breastplate, my sword for the fight, Be Thou my armor, and be Thou my might. Thou my soul's shelter, and Thou my high tower, Raise Thou me heavenward, O Power of my Power!"*

"Aw, for the love o' God woould yoo *hit* the bloody ball!" Archie exploded just as my Maxfli did.

It wasn't a very long drive, but it went heavenward, strraight and trooo. A sight straighter and truer than many of the ones hit by my cantankerous partner, who drove us into Gullane's monster sand traps so many times I seriously considered renaming him Archie Bunker. Nonetheless, he was an excellent sand wedge coach, and with his wise counsel I managed to get us out of trouble each time in one trembling try.

By the time we reached the 7th tee on the top of Gullane Hill, the true spell of Scottish golf had been cast. To the south, the Lammermuir Hills threw a protective arm along the corn and barley fields below. To the north and east, Aberlady Bay glittered its way into the North Sea, stippled with ships and islands. The coastal wind battered our hair and whisked our cheeks as red as children's.

"I can't believe I'm seventy," Bill murmured happily. All I could think to tell him was: "You're not. Not out here you aren't."

The expansive vista, the satisfying alteration between tawny sandlands and green, the pure, wind-wild poetry of the place made golf there seem inevitable. How different this was, how natural, compared with the choreographed terrain of golf courses back home. *This* was golf. *This* was the game as it first knew itself. Gullane, I knew, was golf as it was in the beginning and should be forever more.

After our round, Seonaid and I did what Gullane golfers have done for centuries—we repaired to the men's clubhouse with our hosts. Seonaid had something called a Thistle Ale and I had a scotch, some fragrant blend Archie selected for me, eschewing the drinking of single malts as "unnecessary." We talked the way club members have always talked, of politics and golf swings, even of business.

"Yoo know," Archie offered in a slow conspiratorial voice, "I paid five hundred pounds for the original watercolor of the photograph I have of Old Tom Morris in the museum. We had three kids in paying schools back then. My wife said, 'You're mad!' Then, about five years ago, I sold it to a guy in California for twenty-five thousand pounds!"

"For Old Tom Morris!" I cried out.

"Oh, but don't sell him short," Archie warned. "In 1903 he was prevailed upon to make a speech at the Scottish Ladies'

Championship in St Andrews, and Old Tom said that the ladies deserved 'very great credit' for their play. In *1903!*"

We soon learned that the reason we were allowed to drink and talk with the men at all was due to the early business savvy of the women of the Gullane Ladies' Golf Club.

"The land which the Gullane Ladies' Golf Club acquired for their clubhouse turned out to be far better than the men's," Archie explained. "Finally, the men had to come on bended knee to ask the ladies to let them buy some of their land on which to build a clubhouse. Oh, and the ladies extracted a pretty penny for it, too! AND special rights and privileges as well."

Today, the Gullane ladies' and men's clubhouses are halves of a single, handsome building. The ladies come and go as they please, on both sides, and they have full rights to Gullane No. 1 Course, which was why Seonaid and I had been welcomed to play a round at a prime tee time.

"About your golf," Archie finally said to me, leaning purposefully across the table. "You've got t'learrn t'play better . . . and you've got t'learrn to play *faster.*"

"No," I thought, "I've got t'learrn to play in Scotland."

The spell of Gullane was still upon me when I awoke the next morning. It was early, the skies were a gauzy powder blue, and I wanted to walk the chilled streets of St Andrews one last time before the business of the day overtook them and I left for home.

It felt as though I were walking inside a little cloud of pink fairy dust. The colors seemed saturated, Lede Braes now thin, now thick with quick pockets of morning perfumes, the dark syrup of coffee, the musky sweetness of bacon, the old, old danger-and-safety scent of wood smoke on cold air. Even the familiar pabulum of porridge smelled earthy and exotic in my pixilated state of mind.

Instinctively, I headed for the Old Course. Who wouldn't. The Royal and Ancient pulls you to it by the sheer gravity of history. The frighteningly exposed length of green before it, the daring sea beyond—you have to see them again and again, memorize them, and thereby take them home with you. In the thinning morning harr it all seemed dreamlike, as it undoubtedly has to countless American golfers who have made their own pilgrimages to the stalwart heart of the home of golf.

I turned left down the cobbled skin of the Links Road, past the St Andrews Woollen Mill, past the dear bow window of the St Rule Club. I looked up, hoping to see Joy Steele's wonderful face, but, of course, it was far too early.

My eye crossed the fairway, and through the mist I could barely make out the mini-Himalayas of the Ladies' Putting Club, which bade me think of the ever-spirited Enid Wilson, who, I had learned despite her modesty, had won, in 1931, '32, and '33, three British Women's Amateur Championships in a row. The clubhouse, of course, was as locked up as it had been when Enid had tried to unlock it for us that first day in St Andrews.

As I walked, a man in a kilt strode past me . . . speaking into a cell phone. The only other sign of life seemed to be an inordinate number of crows, one of which suddenly decided to fly perilously close to my head and land boldly on the sacred ground of the 18th, drawing my attention, I must say as if by design, down the fairway.

Then I saw him.

A man. Indistinct and wavering in that coastal veil. He seemed to come in and out of focus as I walked, but two things were sure: He was swinging a golf club and he was wearing what appeared to be a black Stetson.

My step slowed against my bidding. I am sure my mouth made itself into a startled little O. Soon I simply stopped . . . and stared. And when I did, for the life of me, the man stopped, too.

And then he tipped his hat.